Readings in Literary Criticism 16
CRITICS ON SHAKESPEARE

Readings in Literary Criticism

CRITICS ON SHAKESPEARE

Readings in Literary Criticism

Edited by W. T. Andrews

University of the West Indies

London · George Allen & Unwin Ltd

FIRST PUBLISHED IN 1973

© *George Allen & Unwin Ltd* 1973
ISBN 0 04 821034 X

PRINTED IN GREAT BRITAIN
in 10 *on* 11 *pt Plantin type*
BY CLARKE, DOBLE & BRENDON LIMITED
PLYMOUTH

CONTENTS

ACKNOWLEDGEMENTS

We are grateful to the following for permission to use copyright material from the works whose titles follow in brackets:

Clarendon Press, Oxford (Richard G. Moulton's *Shakespeare as a Dramatic Artist* 1901); The Society of Authors on behalf of the Bernard Shaw Estate (Bernard Shaw's Preface to *Three Plays for Puritans*); Macmillan and Company (A. C. Bradley's *Shakespearean Tragedy*, Lecture I 1904; S. Walter Raleigh's *Shakespeare*); Cambridge University Press (Caroline Spurgeon's *Shakespeare's Imagery* and *Shakespeare's Imagery and What it Tells us; Cambridge History of English Literature* Volume V edited by A. W. Ward and A. R. Waller, Chapter 8 by George Saintsbury); Faber and Faber Ltd (T. S. Eliot's *Selected Essays*, 'Hamlet and His Problems'); Gordian Inc., New York (E. E. Stoll's *Hamlet: An Historical and Comparative Study*); B. T. Batsford Ltd (Harley Granville-Barker's *Prefaces to Shakespeare King Lear* and *Antony and Cleopatra* Vols II and III, pp. 1–4, 19 and 5–6); Methuen and Co. Ltd (G. Wilson Knight's *The Wheel of Fire*; W. H. Clemen's *The Development of Shakespeare's Imagery*); Chatto and Windus Ltd (L. C. Knight's *Explorations*, Part One and Part Two of *How Many Children had Lady Macbeth*); Faber and Faber Ltd (John Dover Wilson's *Shakespeare's Happy Comedies*); Cambridge University Press and Mrs Dover Wilson (John Dover Wilson's *What Happens in Hamlet*); Stephen Tillyard and Chatto and Windus Ltd (E. M. W. Tillyard's *Shakespeare's History Plays*, Conclusions 1946); Miss Angela Tillyard and Chatto and Windus Ltd (E. M. W. Tillyard's *Shakespeare's Last Plays*); Prentice-Hall, Inc., Englewood Cliffs, N. J. (*Shakespeare: The Comedies*, edited by Kenneth Muir. Copyright © 1956).

INTRODUCTION

This book lays no claim to be a history or even an anthology of Shakespeare criticism. Perhaps it is hardly necessary to state this, since even a very long book would prove inadequate as a summary of the vast and varied mass of Shakespeare criticism which has accumulated over the centuries, and particularly during our own century. As M. C. Bradbrook has remarked in *Shakespeare Survey 6*, there is now a book or article on Shakespeare published for every day of the year.

The result for the student of Shakespeare is discouraging and confusing. If I may reminisce for a moment, I recall that when I first went up to Cambridge to read English, I was handed a list of some three hundred books on Shakespeare and told to read those for a start. I also recall solving the problem of what to read and of what not to read by throwing away the list and concentrating on reading Shakespeare instead. It would have been useful, however, in order to avoid this drastic treatment of Shakespeare's critics, some of whom have had valuable things to say, to have had a collection of their most notable insights—of the sort usually quoted or referred to from time to time by university teachers—readily available to act as guide-lines to the main critical approaches to Shakespeare through the ages.

That, briefly, is the idea behind this book. The present-day student of Shakespeare, however conscientious he may be, is faced with the problem of economizing somehow. With the best will in the world, he cannot hope to read a thousandth part of all that seriously pretends to be a contribution to Shakespeare studies. He accordingly needs to be given some thread to lead him without undue waste of effort through the maze of Shakespeare criticism. For it *is* waste of effort if the student starts his Shakespearean education by trying to read Shakespeare criticism haphazardly and indiscriminately.

The student needs first to learn where to look, and what to look for. This little book is consequently divided into three parts for the sake of neatness. The first part deals in what is essential in Shakespeare criticism from the time of Shakespeare's contemporaries to the time of Dryden and the Augustans. Shakespeare's contemporaries and early commentators, however critically unsophisticated they were by modern standards, seem at least to have recognized that in Shakespeare they were in contact with a genius *naturally* greater than that of the Ancients taken either singly or combined. When they were not jealous (like Robert Greene), they therefore stressed Shakespeare's universality and his all-comprehensive soul. Yet they were troubled by reverence for the past, by the seeming impossibility of literary greatness in the vernacular, and by the fact that Shakespeare broke most of the rules said to govern poetic drama. There followed, after a period of dislocation and confusion, the curious mixed hostility and enthusiasm of Dryden and the Augustans, Shakespeare emerging in their more refined estimation as a sort of colossal barbarian whose natural powers somehow miraculously triumphed over the bounds of the polite and the correct. This was also the age of Thomas Rymer, who seems to have had no taste whatsoever (he it was who described *Othello* as a 'bloody farce, without salt or savour'), and of the first would-be scholarly emendators and improvers of Shakespeare's texts.

The second part of this rapid survey is concerned with the more introverted and speculative intricacies of nineteenth-century criticism. As early as 1777, in fact, the predominant mode of nineteenth century character-criticism was established with the publication of Maurice Morgann's celebrated *Essay on the Dramatic Character of Sir John Falstaff*. About this time it became the fashion to observe, from an increasingly arm-chair point of view, the psychological depth of Shakespeare's probings into *human* nature (an interest corresponding with the continued rise of the novel, an art-form intimately linked with 'real' or true-to-life characterization).

Twentieth-century Shakespeare criticism, a selection of which concludes this volume, is infinitely more difficult to map with any degree of assurance or justice. But at least this much may emerge for the benefit of students about to enter this maze. Nineteenth century character-criticism, culminating in A. C. Bradley's massive *Shakespearean Tragedy* of 1904, has largely given way to a wider preoccupation with Shakespeare's plays as plays, and with his plays as *poems*. Within the very limited space at my disposal, I have concentrated upon emphasizing this indubitably important aspect of modern Shakespeare studies.

University of the West Indies, 1972   W. T. ANDREWS

Critics on Shakespeare 1592-1777

ROBERT GREENE (1558-92)

... There is an vpstart Crow, beautified with our feathers, that with his *Tygers heart wrapt in a Players hyde*, supposes he is as well able to bombast out a blanke verse as the best of you: and beeing an absolute *Iohannes fac totum*, is in his owne conceit the onely Shake-scene in a countrey.

From *Greenes Groats-worth of Wit*, posthumously published September 1592.

FRANCIS MERES (1565-1647)

As *Plautus* and *Seneca* are accounted the best for Comedy and Tragedy among the Latines: so *Shakespeare* among the English is the most excellent in both kinds for the stage; for Comedy, witnes his *Gentlemen of Verona*, his *Errors*, his *Loue labors lost*, his *Loue labours wonne*, his *Midsummers night dreame*, & his *Merchant of Venice*: for Tragedy his *Richard the 2. Richard the 3. Henry the 4. King Iohn, Titus Andronicus* and his *Romeo and Iuliet*.

As *Epius Stolo* said, that the Muses would speake with Plautus tongue, if they would speak Latin: so I say that the Muses would speake with *Shakespeares* fine filed phrase, if they would speake English. . . .[1]

From *Palladis Tamia: Wits Treasury*, September 1598.

RICHARD BARNFIELD (1574-1627)

A Remembrance of some English Poets

And *Shakespeare* thou, whose hony-flowing Vaine,
(Pleasing the World) thy Praises doth obtaine.

[1] Nevertheless, despite this generous praise, Meres goes on to list Shakespeare in the insignificant company of Doctors Leg and Edes ('These are our best for Tragedie'), and of Doctor Gager and other unknowns ('The best for Comedy amongst us'). (Ed.)

Whose *Venus*, and whose *Lucrece* (sweete, and chaste)
Thy Name in fames immortall Booke haue plac'd.
Liue euer you, at least in Fame liue euer:
Well may the Bodye dye, but Fame dies neuer.

From *Poems in Divers Humors*, 1598.

JOHN WEEVER (1576–1632)

Ad Gulielmum Shakespeare

Honie-tong'd *Shakespeare* when I saw thine issue
I swore *Apollo* got them and none other,
Their rosie-tainted features cloth'd in tissue,
Some heauen born goddesse said to be their mother:
Rose-checkt *Adonis* with his amber tresses,
Faire fire-hot *Venus* charming him to loue her,
Chaste *Lucretia* virgine-like her dresses,
Prowd lust-stung *Tarquine* seeking still to proue her:
Romea Richard; more whose names I know not,
Their sugred tongues, and power attractiue beuty
Say they are Saints althogh that Sts they shew not
For thousands vowes to them subiectiue dutie:
They burn in loue thy children Shakespear het them,
Go, wo thy Muse more Mymphish brood beget them.

From *Epigrammes in the oldest Cut, and newest Fashion*, iv. 22, 1599.

ANON (1599? 1601?)

Gull . . . Let this duncified worlde esteeme of Spencer and Chaucer, I'le worshipp sweet Mr Shakespeare, and to honoure him will lay his Venus and Adonis under my pillowe, as wee reade of one (I doe not well remember his name, but I am sure he was a kinge) slept with Homer under his bed's heade.

Kempe Few of the vniuersity men pen plaies well, they smell too much of that writer *Ouid*, and that writer *Metamorphosis*, and talke too much of *Proserpina* & *Iuppiter*. Why heres our fellow *Shakespeare* puts them all downe, I and *Ben Ionson* too. O that *Ben Ionson* is a pestilent fellow, he brought vp *Horace* giuing the Poets a pill, but our fellow *Shakespeare* hath giuen him a purge that made him beray his credit.

From the *Parnassus* plays, ed. W. D. Macray (1886), severally performed at St John's, Cambridge, probably between 1598 and 1601.

JOHN HEMINGE AND HENRY CONDELL (1556–1630? 1627?)

It had bene a thing, we confesse, worthie to have bene wished, that the Author himselfe had liv'd to have set forth, and overseen his owne writings. But since it hath been ordain'd otherwise, and he by death departed from that right, we pray you do not envie his Friends, the office of their care, and paine, to have collected and publish'd them; and so to have publish'd them, as where (before) you were abused with diverse stolne, and surreptitious copies, maimed, and deformed by the frauds and stealthes of injurious impostors, that expos'd them: even those, are now offer'd to your view cur'd, and perfect of their limbes; and all the rest, absolute in their numbers, as he conceived them. Who, as he was a happie imitator of Nature, was a most gentle expresser of it. His mind and hand went together: And what he thought, he uttered with that easinesse, that wee have scarse received from him a blot in his papers. But it is not our province, who onely gather his works, and give them you, to praise him. It is yours that reade him. And there we hope, to your divers capacities, you will finde enough, both to draw, and hold you: for his wit can no more lie hid, then it could be lost. Reade him, therefore; and againe, and againe: And if then you doe not like him, surely you are in some manifest danger, not to understand him. And so we leave you to other of his Friends, whom if you need, can bee your guides: if you neede them not, you can leade your selves, and others. And such Readers we wish him.

    The prefatory letter addressed 'To the great Variety of Readers' by the Editors of the First Folio, 1623.

BEN JONSON (1573–1637)

To draw no envy (Shakespeare) on thy name,
Am I thus ample to thy Booke, and Fame:
While I confesse thy writings to be such,
As neither *Man*, nor *Muse*, can praise too much.
'Tis true, and all mens suffrage. But these wayes
Were not the paths I meant unto thy praise:
For seeliest Ignorance on these may light,
Which, when it sounds at best, but eccho's right;
Or blinde Affection, which doth ne're advance
The truth, but gropes, and urgeth all by chance;
Or crafty Malice, might pretend this praise,
And thinke to ruine, where it seem'd to raise.
These are, as some infamous Baud, or Whore,
Should praise a Matron. What could hurt her more?
But thou art proofe against them, and indeed
Above th'ill fortune of them, or the need.

I therefore will begin. Soule of the Age!
The applause! delight! the wonder of our Stage!
My *Shakespeare*, rise; I will not lodge thee by
Chaucer, or *Spenser*, or bid *Beaumont* lye
A little further, to make thee a roome:
Thou art a Moniment, without a tombe,
And art alive still, while thy Booke doth live,
And we have wits to read, and praise to give.
That I not mixe thee so, my braine excuses;
I meane with great, but disproportion'd *Muses*:
For, if I thought my judgement were of yeeres,
I should commit thee surely with thy peeres,
And tell, how farre thou didst our *Lily* out-shine,
Or sporting *Kid*, or *Marlowes* mighty line.
And though thou hadst small Latine, and lesse *Greeke*,
From thence to honour thee, I would not seeke
For names; but call forth thund'ring *Aeschilus*,
Euripides, and *Sophocles* to us,
Paccuvius, *Accius*, him of *Cordova* dead,
To life againe, to hear thy Buskin tread,
And shake a Stage: Or, when they Sockes were on,
Leave thee alone, for the comparison
Of all, that insolent *Greece*, or haughtie *Rome*
Sent forth, or since did from their ashes come.
Triumph, my *Britaine*, thou hast one to showe,
To whom all Scenes of *Europe* homage owe.
He was not of an age, but for all time!
And all the *Muses* still were in their prime,
When like *Apollo* he came forth to warme
Our eares, or like a *Mercury* to charme!
Nature her selfe was proud of his designes,
And joy'd to weare the dressing of his lines!
Which were so righly spun, and woven so fit,
As, since, she will vouchsafe no other Wit.
The merry *Greeke*, tart *Aristophanes*,
Neat *Terrence*, witty *Plautus*, now not please;
But antiquated, and deserted lye
As they were not of Natures family.
Yet must I not give Nature all: Thy Art,
My gentle *Shakespeare*, must enjoy a part.
For though the *Poets* matter, *Nature* be,
His Art doth give the fashion. And, that he,
Who casts to write a living line, must sweat,
(Such as thine are) and strike the second heat
Upon the *Muses* anvile: turne the same,
(And himselfe with it) that he thinkes to frame;
Or for the lawrell, he may gaine a scorne,

For a good Poet's made, as well as borne.
And such wert thou. Looke how the fathers face
Lives in his issue, even so, the race
Of *Shakespeares* minde, and manners brightly shines
In his well torned, and true-filed lines:
In each of which, he seemes to shake a Lance,
As brandish't at the eyes of Ignorance.
Sweet Swan of *Avon*! what a sight it were
To see thee in our waters yet appeare,
And make those flights upon the bankes of *Thames*,
That so did take *Eliza*, and our *James*!
But stay, I see thee in the *Hemisphere*
Advanc'd, and made a Constellation there!
Shine forth, thou Starre of *Poets*, and with rage,
Or influence, chide, or cheere the drooping Stage;
Which, since thy flight from hence, hath mourn'd like night,
And despaires day, but for thy Volumes light.

[*Editor's Note : This formal eulogy, whose full title reads 'To the memory of my beloved, The Author Mr William Shakespeare: And What He Hath Left Us', is the most important of several poems of praise preceding the First Folio of Shakespeare's works. On other, less formal occasions, however, Jonson was apt to be more severely critical of what he regarded as Shakespeare's weaknesses as a poet. The above occasional poem therefore needs to be read in conjunction with what follows, belonging to a later date.*]

De Shakespeare nostrati. I remember, the Players have often mentioned it as an honour to *Shakespeare*, that in his writing, (whatsoever he penn'd) hee never blotted out line. My answer hath beene, would he had blotted a thousand. Which they thought a malevolent speech. I had not told posterity this, but for their ignorance, who choose that circumstance to commend their friend by, wherein he most faulted. And to justifie mine owne candor, (for I lov'd the man, and doe honour his memory (on this side Idolatry) as much as any.) Hee was (indeed) honest, and of an open, and free nature: had an excellent *Phantsie*; brave notions, and gentle expressions: wherein hee flow'd with that facility, that sometime it was necessary he should be stop'd: *Sufflaminandus erat*; as *Augustus* said of *Haterius*. His wit was in his owne power; would the rule of it had beene so too. Many times hee fell into those things, could not escape laughter: As when hee said in the person of *Caesar*, one speaking to him; *Caesar thou dost me wrong*. Hee replyed: *Caesar did never wrong, but with just cause*: and such like, which were ridiculous. But he redeemed his vices, with his vertues. There was ever more in him to be praysed, then to be pardoned.

From *Timber: or, Discoveries*, 1641. See Bodley Head Quartos V, ed. G. B. Harrison, p. 28.

JOHN DRYDEN (1631–1700)

He was the man who of all modern, and perhaps ancient, poets, had the largest and most comprehensive soul. All the images of nature were still present to him, and he drew them, not laboriously, but luckily; when he describes anything, you more than see it, you feel it too. Those who accuse him to have wanted learning give him the greater commendation: he was naturally learned; he needed not the spectacles of books to read nature; he looked inwards and found her there. I cannot say he is everywhere alike; were it so, I should do him injury to compare him with the greatest of mankind. He is many times flat, insipid; his comic wit degenerating into clenches, his serious swelling into bombast. But he is always great, when some great occasion is presented to him.

From the *Essay of Dramatic Poesy*, 1668.

The poet Aeschylus was held in the same veneration by the Athenians of after ages as Shakespeare is by us; and Longinus has judged, in favour of him, that he had a noble boldness of expression, and that his imaginations were lofty and heroic; but, on the other side, Quintilian affirms that he was daring to extravagance. 'Tis certain that he affected pompous words, and that his sense was too often obscured by figures; notwithstanding these imperfections, the value of his writings after his decease was such, that his countrymen ordained an equal reward to those poets who could alter this plays to be acted on the theatre, with those whose productions were wholly new, and of their own. The case is not the same in England; though the difficulties of altering are greater, and our reverence for Shakespeare much more just, than that of the Grecians for Aeschylus. In the age of that poet, the Greek tongue was arrived to its full perfection; they had then amongst them an exact standard of writing and of speaking: the English language is not capable of such a certainty; and we are at present so far from it, that we are wanting in the very foundation of it, a perfect grammar. Yet it must be allowed to the present age, that the tongue in general is so much refined since Shakespeare's time, that many of his words, and more of his phrases, are scarce intelligible. And of those which we understand, some are ungrammatical, others coarse; and his whole style is so pestered with figurative expressions, that it is as affected as it is obscure. 'Tis true, that in his later plays he had worn off somewhat of the rust; but the tragedy which I have undertaken to correct was in all probability one of his first endeavours on the stage.

From the opening paragraph of the Preface to Dryden's revised version of *Troilus and Cressida*, 1679.

If Shakespeare be allowed, as I think he must, to have made his characters distinct, it will easily be inferred that he understood the nature of the passions: because it has been proved already that confused passions make undistinguishable characters: yet I cannot deny that he has his failings; but they are not so much in the passions themselves, as in his manner of expression: he often obscures his meaning by his words, and sometimes makes it unintelligible. I will not say of so great a poet, that he distinguished not the blown puffy style from true sublimity; but I may venture to maintain, that the fury of his fancy often transported him beyond the bounds of judgment, either in coining of new words and phrases, or racking words which were in use, into the violence of a catachresis. It is not that I would explode the use of metaphors from passion, for Longinus thinks 'em necessary to raise it: but to use 'em at every word, to say nothing without a metaphor, a simile, an image, or description, is, I doubt, to smell a little too strongly of the buskin. I must be forced to give an example of expressing passion figuratively; but that I may do it with respect to Shakespeare, it shall not be taken from anything of his: 'tis an exclamation against Fortune, quoted in his *Hamlet* but written by some other poet—

Out, out, thou strumpet, Fortune! all you gods,
In general synod, take away her power;
Break all the spokes and felleys from her wheel,
And bowl the round nave down the hill of Heav'n,
As low as to the fiends.

And immediately after, speaking of Hecuba, when Priam was killed before her eyes—

The mobled queen
Threatning the flame, ran up and down
With bisson rheum; a clout about that head
Where late the diadem stood; and for a robe,
About her lank and all o'er-teemed loins,
A blanket in th'alarm of fear caught up.
Who this had seen, with tongue in venom steep'd
'Gainst Fortune's state would treason have pronounced;
But if the gods themselves did see her then,
When she saw Pyrrhus make malicious sport
In mincing with his sword her husband's limbs,
The instant burst of clamour that she made
(Unless things mortal move them not at all)
Would have made milch the burning eyes of heaven,
And passion in the gods.

What a pudder is here kept in raising the expression of trifling thoughts! Would not a man have thought that the poet had been bound prentice to a wheelwright, for his first rant? and had followed a rag-man, for the clout and blanket in the second? Fortune is painted on a wheel, and therefore the writer, in a rage, will have poetical justice done upon every member of that engine: after this execution, he bowls the nave down-hill, from Heaven, to the fiends (an unreasonable long mark, a man would think); 'tis well there are no solid orbs to stop it in the way, or no element of fire to consume it: but when it came to the earth, it must be monstrous heavy, to break ground as low as the centre. His making milch the burning eyes of heaven was a pretty tolerable flight too: and I think no man ever drew milk out of eyes before him: yet, to make the wonder greater, these eyes were burning. Such a sight indeed were enough to have raised passion in the gods; but to excuse the effects of it, he tells you, perhaps they did not see it. Wise men would be glad to find a little sense couched under all these pompous words; for bombast is commonly the delight of that audience which loves Poetry, but understands it not: and as commonly has been the practice of those writers, who, not being able to infuse a natural passion into the mind, have made it their business to ply the ears, and to stun their judges by the noise. But Shakespeare does not often thus; for the passions in his scene between Brutus and Cassius are extremely natural, the thoughts are such as arise from the matter, the expression of 'em not viciously figurative. I cannot leave this subject, before I do justice to that divine poet, by giving you one of his passionate descriptions: 'tis of Richard the Second when he was deposed, and led in triumph through the streets of London by Henry of Bullingbrook: the painting of it is so lively, and the words so moving, that I have scarce read anything comparable to it in any other language. Suppose you have seen already the fortunate usurper passing through the crowd, and followed by the shouts and acclamations of the people; and now behold King Richard entering upon the scene: consider the wretchedness of his condition, and his carriage in it; and refrain from pity, if you can—

> As in a theatre, the eyes of men,
> After a well-graced actor leaves the stage,
> Are idly bent on him that enters next,
> Thinking his prattle to be tedious:
> Even so, or with much more contempt, men's eyes
> Did scowl on Richard: no man cried, God save him:
> No joyful tongue gave him his welcome home,
> But dust was thrown upon his sacred head,
> Which with such gentle sorrow he shook off,
> His face still combating with tears and smiles
> (The badges of his grief and patience),
> That had not God (for some strong purpose) steel'd
> The hearts of men, they must perforce have melted,
> And barbarism itself have pitied him.

To speak justly of this whole matter: 'tis neither height of thought that is discommended, nor pathetic vehemence, nor any nobleness of expression in its proper place; but 'tis a false measure of all these, something which is like them, and is not them; 'tis the Bristol-stone, which appears like a diamond; 'tis an extravagant thought, instead of a

sublime one; 'tis roaring madness, instead of vehemence; and a sound
of words, instead of sense. If Shakespeare were stripped of all the
bombasts in his passions, and dressed in the most vulgar words, we
should find the beauties of his thoughts remaining; if his embroideries
were burnt down, there would still be silver at the bottom of the
melting-pot: but I fear (at least let me fear it for myself) that we, who
ape his sounding words, have nothing of his thought, but are all outside;
there is not so much as a dwarf within our giant's clothes. Therefore,
let not Shakespeare suffer for our sakes; 'tis our fault, who succeed
him in an age which is more refined, if we imitate him so ill, that we
copy his failings only, and make a virtue of that in our writings which
in his was an imperfection.

From the final section of the Preface to *Troilus and Cressida*, entitled
'The Grounds of Criticism in Tragedy'.

Shakespeare, who many times has written better than any poet, in any
language, is yet so far from writing wit always, or expressing that wit
according to the dignity of the subject, that he writes, in many places,
below the dullest writer of ours, or any precedent age. Never did any
author precipitate himself from such height of thought to so low
expressions, as he often does. He is the very Janus of poets; he wears
almost everywhere two faces; and you have scarce begun to admire
the one, ere you despise the other.

From the *Essay on the Dramatique Poetry of the Last Age*, 1672.

THOMAS RYMER (1641-1713)

From all the Tragedies acted on our English Stage, *Othello* is said to
bear the Bell away. The *Subject* is more of a piece, and there is indeed
something like, there is, as it were, some phantom of a *Fable*. The
Fable is always accounted the *Soul* of Tragedy. And it is the *Fable*
which is properly the *Poets* part. Because the other three parts of
Tragedy, to wit the *Characters* are taken from the Moral Philosopher;
the *thoughts* or sence, from them that teach *Rhetorick*: And the last part,
which is the *expression*, we learn from the Grammarians.
   This Fable is drawn from a Novel, compos'd in Italian by *Giraldi
Cinthio*, who also was a Writer of Tragedies. And to that use employ'd
such of his Tales, as he judged proper for the Stage. But with this of
the *Moor*, he meddl'd no farther.
   Shakespeare alters it from the Original in several particulars, but
always, unfortunately, for the worse. He bestows a name on his *Moor*,
and styles him the Moor of *Venice*: a Note of pre-eminence, which
neither History nor Heraldry can allow him. *Cinthio*, who knew him
best, and whose creature he was, calls him simply a *Moor*. We say the

Piper of *Strasburgh*; the Jew of *Florence*; And, if you please, the Pindar of *Wakefield*: all upon Record, and memorable in their Places. But we see no such Cause for the *Moors* preferment to that dignity. And it is an affront to all Chroniclers, and Antiquaries, to top upon 'um a *Moor*, with that mark of renown, who yet had never faln within the Sphere of their Cognisance.

Then is the Moors *Wife*, from a simple Citizen in *Cinthio*, dress'd up with her Top knots, and rais'd to be *Desdemona*, a Senators Daughter. All this is very strange; And therefore pleases such as reflect not on the probability. This match might well be without the Parents Consent. Old Horace long ago forbad the Banes.

Sed non ut placidis Coeant immitia, non ut
Serpentes avibus geminentur, tigribus agni.
[But not that the savage should join with the gentle,
nor serpents with savages, nor lambs with tigers.]

Horace, Art of Poetry, ll. 12–13

What ever rubs or difficulty may stick on the Bark, the Moral, sure, of this *Fable* is very instructive.

I. First, This may be a caution to all Maidens of Quality how, without their Parents consent, they run away with Blackamoors.

Di non si accompagnare con huomo, cui la natura e il cielo, e il modo della vita, disgiunge da noi. Cinthio. [Not to go with a man whom nature and heaven and manner of life separate from us.]

Secondly, This may be a warning to all good Wives, that they look well to their Linnen.

Thirdly. This may be a lesson to Husbands, that before their jealousie be Tragical, the proofs may be Mathematical.

. . . *Shakespears* genius lay for Comedy and Humour. In Tragedy he appears quite out of his Element; his Brains are turn'd, he raves and rambles, without any coherence, any spark of reason, or any rule to controul him, or set bounds to his phrenzy . . .

The Italian Painters are noted for drawing the *Madonna's* by their own Wives or Mistresses; one might wonder what sort of *Betty Mackerel*, *Shakespear* found in his days, to sit for his *Portia*, and *Desdemona*; and Ladies of a rank, and dignity, for their place in Tragedy. But to him a Tragedy in *Burlesk*, a merry Tragedy, was no Monster, no absurdity, nor at all preposterous: all colours are the same to a Blind man.

. . . To gain attention *Aristotle* told us, it was necessary that an Orator be a *good Man*; therefore he that writes Tragedy should be careful that the persons of his *Drama*, be of consideration and importance, that the *Audience* may readily lend an Ear, and give attention to what they say, and act. Who would thrust into a crowd to hear what Mr *Iago*, *Roderigo*, or *Cassio*, is like to say? From a Venetian Senate, or a Roman Senate one might expect great matters: But their Poet was out of sorts; he had it not for them; the Senators must be no wiser than other folk.

Ben. Johnson, knew how to distinguish men and manners, at another rate. In *Catiline* we find our selves in *Europe*, we are no longer in the *Land of Savages*, amongst Blackamoors, Barbarians, and Monsters.

From *A Short View of Tragedy; It's Original, Excellency, and Corruption. With some Reflections on Shakespear, and other Practitioners for the Stage*, 1693.

NICHOLAS ROWE (1674–1718)

As I have not propos'd to my self to enter into a Large and Compleat Criticism upon Mr *Shakespear's* Works, so I suppose it will neither be expected that I should take notice of the severe Remarks that have been formerly made upon him by Mr *Rhymer*. I must confess, I can't very well see what could be the Reason of his animadverting with so much Sharpness, upon the Faults of a Man Excellent on most Occasions, and whom all the World ever was and will be inclin'd to have an Esteem and Veneration for. If it was to shew his own Knowledge in the Art of Poetry, besides that there is a Vanity in making that only his Design, I question if there be not many Imperfections as well in those Schemes and Precepts he has given for the Direction of others, as well as in that Sample of Tragedy which he has written to shew the Excellency of his own *Genius*. If he had a Pique against the Man, and wrote on purpose to ruin a Reputation so well establish'd, he has had the Mortification to fail altogether in his Attempt, and to see the World at least as fond of *Shakespear* as of his Critique. But I won't believe a Gentleman, and a good-natur'd Man, capable of the last Intention. Whatever may have been his Meaning, finding fault is certainly the easiest Task of Knowledge, and commonly those Men of good Judgment, who are likewise of good and gentle Dispositions, abandon this ungrateful Province to the Tyranny of Pedants. If one would enter into the Beauties of *Shakespear*, there is a much larger, as well as a more delightful Field; but as I won't prescribe to the tastes of other People, so I will only take the liberty, with all due Submission to the Judgment of others, to observe some of those Things I have been pleas'd with in looking him over.

His Plays are properly to be distinguish'd only into Comedies and Tragedies. Those which are called Histories, and even some of his Comedies, are really Tragedies, with a run or mixture of Comedy amongst 'em. That way of Trage-Comedy was the common Mistake of that Age, and is indeed become so agreeable to the *English* Tast, that tho' the severer Critiques among us cannot bear it, yet the generality of our Audiences seem to be better pleas'd with it than with an exact Tragedy. *The Merry Wives of Windsor*, *The Comedy of Errors*, and *The Taming of the Shrew*, are all pure Comedy; the rest, however they are call'd, have something of both Kinds. 'Tis not very easie to determine which way of Writing he was most Excellent in.

It is the same Magick that raises the Fairies in *Midsummer Night's Dream*, the Witches in *Macbeth*, and the Ghost in *Hamlet*, with Thoughts and Language so proper to the Parts they sustain, and so peculiar to the Talent of this Writer. But of the two last of these Plays I shall have occasion to take notice, among the Tragedies of Mr *Shakespear*. If one undertook to examine the greatest part of these by those Rules which are establish'd by *Aristotle*, and taken from the Model of the *Grecian* Stage, it would be no very hard Task to find a great many Faults: But as *Shakespear* liv'd under a kind of mere Light of Nature, and had never been made acquainted with the Regularity of those written Precepts, so it would be hard to judge him by a Law he knew nothing of. We are to consider him as a Man that liv'd in a State of almost universal License and Ignorance: There was no establish'd Judge, but every one took the liberty to Write according to the Dictates of his own Fancy. When one considers, that there is not one Play before him of a Reputation good enough to entitle it to an Appearance on the present Stage, it cannot but be a Matter of great Wonder that he should advance Dramatick Poetry as far as he did.

. . . Since I had at first resolv'd not to enter into any Critical Controversie, I won't pretend to enquire into the Justness of Mr *Rhymer's* Remarks on *Othello*; he has certainly pointed out some Faults very judiciously; and indeed they are such as most People will agree, with him, to be Faults: But I wish he would likewise have observ'd some of the Beauties too; as I think it became an Exact and Equal Critique to do. It seems strange that he should allow nothing Good in the whole: If the Fable and Incidents are not to his Taste, yet the Thoughts are almost every where very Noble, and the Diction manly and proper. These last, indeed, are Parts of *Shakespear's* Praise, which it would be very hard to Dispute with him. His Sentiments and Images of Things are Great and Natural; and his Expression (tho' perhaps in some Instances a little Irregular) just, and rais'd in Proportion to his Subject and Occasion. It would be even endless to mention the particular Instances that might be given of this Kind: But his Book is in the Possession of the Publick, and 'twill be hard to dip into any Part of it, without finding what I have said of him made good.

From *Some Account of the Life, etc., of Mr William Shakespeare*, 1709. (The *Account* served as the preface to Rowe's Edition of Shakespeare.)

JOHN DENNIS (1657–1734)

I HERE send you the Tragedy of *Coriolanus*, which I have alter'd from the Original of *Shakespear*, and with it a short Account of the Genius and Writings of that Author. . .

Shakespear was one of the greatest Genius's that the World e'er saw for the Tragick Stage. Tho' he lay under greater Disadvantages than any of his Successors, yet had he greater and more genuine Beauties than the best and greatest of them. And what makes the brightest Glory of his Character, those Beauties were entirely his own, and owing to the Force of his own Nature; whereas his Faults were owing to his Education, and to the Age that he liv'd in. One may say of him as they did of *Homer*, that he had none to imitate, and is himself inimitable. His Imaginations were often as just, as they were bold and strong. He had a natural Discretion which never cou'd have been taught him, and his Judgment was strong and penetrating. He seems to have wanted nothing but Time and Leisure for Thought, to have found out those Rules of which he appears so ignorant. His Characters are always drawn justly, exactly, graphically, except where he fail'd by not knowing History of the Poetical Art. He has for the most part more fairly distinguish'd them than any of his Successors have done, who have falsified them, or confounded them, by making Love the predominant Quality in all. He had so fine a Talent for touching the Passions, and they are so lively, and so truly in Nature, that they often touch us more without their due Preparations, than those of other Tragick Poets, who have all the Beauty of Design and all the Advantage of Incidents. His Master-Passion was Terror, which he has often mov'd so powerfully and so wonderfully, that we may justly conclude, that if he had had the Advantage of Art and Learning, he wou'd have surpass'd the very best and strongest of the Ancients . . .

If *Shakespear* had these great Qualities by Nature, what would he not have been, if he had join'd to so happy a Genius Learning and the Poetical Art? For want of the latter, our Author has sometimes made gross Mistakes in the Characters which he has drawn from History, against the Equality and Conveniency of Manners of his Dramatical Persons. Witness *Menenius* in the following Tragedy, whom he has made an errant Buffoon, which is a great Absurdity. For he might as well have imagin'd a grave majestick *Jack-Pudding*, as a Buffoon in a *Roman* Senator. *Aufidius* the General of the *Volscians* is shewn a base and a profligate Villain. He has offended against the Equality of the Manners even in his Hero himself. For *Coriolanus* who in the first part of the Tragedy is shewn so open, so frank, so violent, and so magnanimous, is represented in the latter part by *Aufidius*, which is contradicted by no one, a flattering, fawning, cringing, insinuating Traytor.

For want of this Poetical Art, *Shakespear* has introduced things into his Tragedies, which are against the Dignity of that noble Poem, as the Rabble in *Julius Caesar*, and that in *Coriolanus*; tho' that in *Coriolanus* offends not only against the Dignity of Tragedy, but against the Truth of History likewise, and the Customs of Ancient *Rome*, and the Majesty of the *Roman* People, as we shall have occasion to shew anon.

For want of this Art, he has made his Incidents less moving, less surprizing, and less wonderful. He has been so far from seeking those fine Occasions to move with which an Action furnish'd according to Art would have furnish'd him, that he seems rather to have industriously avoided them. He makes *Coriolanus*, upon his Sentence of Banishment, take his leave of his Wife and his Mother out of sight of the Audience, and so has purposely as it were avoided a great occasion to move.

If we are willing to allow that *Shakespear*, by sticking to the bare Events of History, has mov'd more than any of his Successors, yet his just Admirers must confess, that if he had had the Poetical Art, he would have mov'd ten times more. For 'tis impossible that by a bare Historical Play he could move so much as he would have done by a Fable.

Tho' *Shakespear* succeeded very well in Comedy, yet his principal Talent and his chief Delight was Tragedy.

From Letters I and III of *On the Genius and Writings of Shakespeare*, 1712.

JOSEPH ADDISON (1672-1719)

... our Criticks do not seem sensible that there is more Beauty in the works of a great Genius who is ignorant of the Rules of Art, than in those of a little Genius who knows and observes them ... Our inimitable *Shakespear* is a Stumbling-block to the whole Tribe of these rigid Criticks. Who would not rather read one of his Plays, where there is not a single Rule of the Stage observed, than any Production of a modern Critick, where there is not one of them violated? *Shakespear* was indeed born with all the Seeds of Poetry, and may be compared to the Stone in *Pyrrhus's* Ring, which, as *Pliny* tells us, had the Figure of *Apollo* and the Nine Muses in the Veins of it, produced by the spontaneous Hand of Nature, without any Help from Art.

From *The Spectator*, No. 592, Friday 10 September, 1714.

ALEXANDER POPE (1688-1744)

If ever any Author deserved the name of an *Original*, it was *Shakespear*. *Homer* himself drew not his art so immediately from the fountains of Nature, it proceeded thro' *Aegyptian* strainers and channels, and came to him not without some tincture of the learning, or some cast of the models, of those before him. The Poetry of *Shakespear* was Inspiration indeed: he is not so much an Imitator, as an Instrument, of Nature; and 'tis not so just to say that he speaks from her, as that she speaks thro' him.

His *Characters* are so much Nature her self, that 'tis a sort of injury to call them by so distant a name as Copies of her. Those of other Poets have a constant resemblance, which shews that they receiv'd them from one another, and were but multiplyers of the same image: each picture like a mock-rainbow is but the reflexion of a reflexion. But every single character in *Shakespear* is as much an Individual as those in Life itself; it is as impossible to find any two alike; and such as from their relation or affinity in any respect appear most to be Twins, will upon comparison be found remarkably distinct. To this life and variety of Character, we must add the wonderful Preservation of it; which is such throughout his plays, that had all the Speeches been printed without the very names of the Persons, I believe one might have apply'd them with certainty to every speaker.

The *Power* over our *Passions* was never possess'd in a more eminent degree, or display'd in so different instances. Yet all along, there is seen no labour, no pains to raise them; no preparation to guide our guess to the effect, or be perceiv'd to lead toward it: But the heart swells, and the tears burst out, just at the proper places: We are surpriz'd, the moment we weep; and yet upon reflection find the passion so just, that we shou'd be surpriz'd if we had not wept, and wept at that very moment . . .

Nor does he only excell in the Passions: In the coolness of Reflection and Reasoning he is full as admirable. His *Sentiments* are not only in general the most pertinent and judicious upon every subject; but by a talent very peculiar, something between Penetration and Felicity, he hits upon that particular point on which the bent of each argument turns, or the force of each motive depends. This is perfectly amazing, from a man of no education or experience in those great and publick scenes of life which are usually the subject of his thoughts: So that he seems to have known the world by Intuition, to have look'd thro' humane nature at one glance, and to be the only Author that gives ground for a very new opinion, That the Philosopher and even the Man of the world, may be *Born,* as well as the Poet.

To judge . . . of *Shakespear* by *Aristotle's* rules, is like trying a man by the Laws of one Country, who acted under those of another. He writ to the *People*; and writ at first without patronage from the better sort, and therefore without aims of pleasing them: without assistance or advice from the Learned, as without the advantage of education or acquaintance among them: without that knowledge of the best models, the Ancients, to inspire him with an emulation of them; in a word, without any views of Reputation, and of what Poets are pleas'd to call Immortality: Some or all of which have encourag'd the vanity, or animated the ambition, of other writers.

From the Preface to *The Works of Shakespear*, 1725.

LEWIS THEOBALD (1688-1744)

As I have never propos'd to dilate farther on the Character of my Author, than was necessary to explain the Nature and Use of this Edition, I shall proceed to consider him as a Genius in Possession of an

everlasting Name. And how great that Merit must be, which could gain
it against all the Disadvantages of the horrid Condition in which he has
hitherto appear'd! Had *Homer*, or any other admir'd Author, first
started into Publick so maim'd and deform'd, we cannot determine
whether they had not sunk for ever under the Ignominy of such an
ill Appearance. The mangled Condition of *Shakespeare* has been
acknowledg'd by Mr *Rowe*, who publish'd him indeed, but neither
corrected his Text, nor collated the old Copies. This Gentleman had
Abilities, and a sufficient Knowledge of his Author, had but his Industry
been equal to his Talents. The same mangled Condition has been
acknowleg'd by Mr *Pope*, who publish'd him likewise, pretended to
have collated the old Copies, and yet seldom has corrected the Text
but to its Injury. I congratulate with the *Manes* of our Poet, that this
Gentleman has been sparing in *indulging his private Sense*, as he phrases
it; for He, who tampers with an Author whom he does not understand,
must do it at the Expence of his Subject. I have made it evident throughout my Remarks, that he has frequently inflicted a Wound where he
intended a Cure . . . He has attack'd him like an unhandy *Slaughterman*;
and not lopp'd off the *Errors*, but the *Poet*.

When this is found to be the Fact, how absurd must appear the
Praises of such an Editor? It seems a moot Point, whether Mr *Pope* has
done most injury to *Shakespeare* as his Editor and Encomiast; or Mr
Rymer done him Service as his Rival and Censurer. They have Both
shewn themselves in an equal *Impuissance* of suspecting, or amending,
the corrupted Passages . . .

It is not with any secret Pleasure, that I so frequently animadvert on
Mr *Pope* as a Critick; but there are Provocations, which a Man can
never quite forget. His Libels have been thrown out with so much
Inveteracy, that, not to dispute whether they *should* come from a
Christian, they leave it a Question whether they *could* come from a
Man . . . It is certain, I am indebted to Him for some *flagrant Civilities*;
and I shall willingly devote a part of my Life to the honest Endeavour
of quitting Scores: with this Exception, however, that I will not
return those Civilities in his *peculiar* Strain, but confine myself, at least,
to the Limits of *common Decency*. I shall ever think it better to want
Wit, than to want *Humanity*: and impartial Posterity may, perhaps, be
of my Opinion.[2]

From the Preface to *The Works of Shakespeare*, 1733.

WILLIAM WARBURTON (1698–1779)

But nothing will give the common Reader a better Idea of the Value of
Mr *Pope's* Edition, than the two Attempts which have been since made,

[2] Posterity has not, on the whole, been of Theobald's opinion. It has generally
sided with Dr Johnson, who described him, despite his careful scholarship, as
'a man of heavy diligence, with very slender powers'.

by Mr *Theobald* and Sir *Thomas Hanmer*,[3] in Opposition to it. Who, altho' they concerned themselves only in the *first* of these three Parts of Criticism, the *restoring the Text* (without any Conception of the *second*, or venturing even to touch upon the *third*)[4] yet succeeded so very ill in it, that they left their Author in ten times a worse Condition than they found him. But, as it was my ill Fortune to have some accidental Connexions with these two *Gentlemen*, it will be incumbent on me to be a little more particular concerning them.

The One was recommended to me as a poor Man; the Other as a poor Critic: and to each of them, at different times, I communicated a great number of Observations, which they managed, as they saw fit, to the Relief of their several Distresses. As to Mr *Theobald*, who wanted Money, I allowed him to print what I gave him for his own Advantage: and he allowed himself in the Liberty of taking one Part for his own, and sequestering another for the Benefit, as I supposed, of some future Edition. But, as to the *Oxford Editor*, who wanted nothing but what he might very well be without, the Reputation of a Critic, I could not so easily forgive him for trafficking with my Papers without my Knowledge; and, when that Project fail'd, for employing a number of my Conjectures in his Edition against my express Desire not to have that Honour done unto me.

Mr *Theobald* was naturally turned to Industry and Labour. What he read he could transcribe: but, as what he thought, if ever he did think, he could but ill express, so he read on; and by that means got a Character of Learning, without risquing, to every Observer, the Imputation of wanting a better Talent. By a punctilious Collation of the old Books, he corrected what was manifestly wrong in the *latter* Editions, by what was manifestly right in the *earlier*. And this is his real merit; and the whole of it. For where the Phrase was very obsolete or licentious in the *common* Books, or only slightly corrupted in the *other*, he wanted sufficient Knowledge of the Progress and various Stages of the *English* Tongue, as well as Acquaintance with the *Peculiarity* of *Shakespear's* Language, to understand what was right; nor had he either common Judgement to see, or critical Sagacity to amend, what was manifestly faulty. Hence he generally exerts his conjectural Talent in the wrong Place: He tampers with what is sound in the *common* Books; and, in the *old* ones, omits all Notice of *Variations* the Sense of which he did not understand.

From the Preface to *The Works of Shakespear*, 1747.

[3] Sir Thomas Hanmer's Edition of Shakespeare appeared in 1744. Hanmer, an ex-Speaker of the House of Commons, relied heavily upon the work of Pope and Theobald for his expensive Edition, as well as making use of the suggestions of Warburton himself.

[4] The second and third Parts of Criticism, according to Warburton, involve 'explaining' Shakespeare's 'licentious Phraseology and obscure Allusions', and 'illustrating the Beauties of his Poetry'.

SAMUEL JOHNSON (1709–1784)

When Learning's triumph o'er her barb'rous foes
First rear'd the stage, immortal Shakespeare rose;
Each change of many-color'd life he drew,
Exhausted worlds, and then imagin'd new:
Existence saw him spurn her bounded reign,
And panting Time toil'd after him in vain:
His pow'rful strokes presiding Truth impress'd,
And unresisted Passion storm'd the Breast.

Prologue Spoken by Mr Garrick at the Opening of the Theatre in Drury-Lane, 1747.

Shakespeare is above all writers, at least above all modern writers, the poet of nature; the poet that holds up to his readers a faithful mirrour of manners and of life. His characters are not modified by the customs of particular places, unpractised by the rest of the world; by the peculiarities of studies or professions, which can operate but upon small numbers; or by the accidents of transient fashions or temporary opinions: they are the genuine progeny of common humanity, such as the world will always supply, and observation will always find. His persons act and speak by the influence of those general passions and principles by which all minds are agitated, and the whole system of life is continued in motion. In the writings of other poets a character is too often an individual; in those of *Shakespeare* it is commonly a species . . .

Other dramatists can only gain attention by hyperbolical or aggravated characters, by fabulous or unexampled excellence or depravity, as the writers of barbarous romances invigorated the reader by a giant and a dwarf; and he that should form his expectations of human affairs from the play, or from the tale, would be equally deceived. *Shakespeare* has no heroes; his scenes are occupied only by men, who act and speak as the reader thinks that he should himself have spoken or acted on the same occasion: Even where the agency is supernatural the dialogue is level with life. Other writers disguise the most natural passions and most frequent incidents; so that he who contemplates them in the book will not know them in the world: Shakespeare approximates the remote, and familiarizes the wonderful; the event which he represents will not happen, but if it were possible, its effects would probably be such as he has assigned; and it may be said, that he has not only shewn human nature as it acts in real exigences, but as it would be found in trials, to which it cannot be exposed.

This therefore is the praise of *Shakespeare*, that his drama is the mirrour of life; that he who has mazed his imagination, in following the phantoms which other writers raise up before him, may here be cured of his delirious extasies, by reading human sentiments in human language; by scenes from which a hermit may estimate the transactions of the world, and a confessor predict the progress of the passions.

His adherence to general nature has exposed him to the censure of criticks, who form their judgments upon narrower principles. *Dennis* and *Rhymer* think his *Romans* not sufficiently *Roman*; and *Voltaire* censures his kings as not completely royal. *Dennis* is offended, that *Menenius*, a Senator of *Rome*, should play the buffoon; and *Voltaire* perhaps thinks decency violated when the *Danish* Usurper is represented as a drunkard. But *Shakespeare* always makes nature predominate over accident; and if he preserves the essential character, is not very careful of distinctions superinduced and adventitious. His story requires Romans or kings, but he thinks only on men. He knew that *Rome*, like every other city, had men of all dispositions; and wanting a buffoon, he went into the senate-house for that which the senate-house would certainly have afforded him. He was inclined to shew an usurper and a murderer not only odious but despicable, he therefore added drunkenness to his other qualities, knowing that kings love wine like other men, and that wine exerts its natural power upon kings. These are the petty cavils of petty minds; a poet overlooks the casual distinction of country and condition, as a painter, satisfied with the figure, neglects the drapery.

The censure which he has incurred by mixing comick and tragick scenes, as it extends to all his works, deserves more consideration. Let the fact be first stated, and then examined.

Shakespeare's plays are not in the rigorous and critical sense either tragedies or comedies, but compositions of a distinct kind; exhibiting the real state of sublunary nature, which partakes of good and evil, joy and sorrow, mingled with endless variety of proportion and innumerable modes of combination; and expressing the course of the world, in which the loss of one is the gain of another; in which, at the same time, the reveller is hasting to his wine, and the mourner burying his friend; in which the malignity of one is sometimes defeated by the frolick of another; and many mischiefs and many benefits are done and hindered without design.

Out of this chaos of mingled purposes and casualties the ancient poets, according to the laws which custom had prescribed, selected some the crimes of men, and some their absurdities; some the momentous vicissitudes of life, and some the lighter occurrences; some the terrours of distress, and some the gayeties of prosperity. Thus rose the two modes of imitation, known by the names of *tragedy* and *comedy*, compositions intended to promote different ends by contrary means, and considered as so little allied, that I do not recollect among the *Greeks* or *Romans* a single writer who attempted both.

Shakespeare has united the powers of exciting laughter and sorrow not only in one mind, but in one composition. Almost all his plays are divided between serious and ludicrous characters, and, in the successive evolutions of the design, sometimes produce seriousness and sorrow, and sometimes levity and laughter.

That this is a practice contrary to the rules of criticism will be readily allowed; but there is always an appeal open from criticism to nature. The end of writing is to instruct; the end of poetry is to instruct by pleasing. That the mingled drama may convey all the instruction of tragedy or comedy cannot be denied, because it includes both in its alternations of exhibition, and approaches nearer than either to the appearance of life, by shewing how great machinations and slender designs may promote or obviate one another, and the high and the low co-operate in the general system by unavoidable concatenation.

It is objected, that by this change of scenes the passions are interrupted in their progression, and that the principal event, being not advanced by a due gradation of preparatory incidents, wants at last the power to move which constitutes the perfection of dramatick poetry. This reasoning is so specious, that it is received as true even by those who in daily experience feel it to be false. The interchanges of mingled scenes seldom fail to produce the intended vicissitudes of passion. Fiction cannot move so much, but that the attention may be easily transferred; and though it must be allowed that pleasing melancholy be sometimes interrupted by unwelcome levity, yet let it be considered likewise, that melancholy is often not pleasing, and the disturbance of one man may be the relief of another; that different auditors have different habitudes; and that, upon the whole, all pleasure consists in variety . . .

When *Shakespeare's* plan is understood, most of the criticisms of *Rhymer* and *Voltaire* vanish away. The play of *Hamlet* is opened, without impropriety, by two sentinels; *Iago* bellows at *Brabantio's* window, without injury to the scheme of the play, though in terms which a modern audience would not easily endure; the character of *Polonius* is seasonable and useful; and the Grave-diggers themselves may be heard with applause.

Shakespeare engaged in dramatick poetry with the world open before him; the rules of the ancients were yet known to few; the publick judgment was unformed; he had no example of such fame as might force him upon imitation, nor criticks of such authority as might restrain his extravagance: He therefore indulged his natural disposition, and his disposition, as *Rhymer* has remarked, led him to comedy. In tragedy he often writes with great appearance of toil and study, what is written at last with little felicity; but in his comick scenes, he seems to produce without labour, what no labour can improve. In tragedy he is always struggling after some occasion to be comick, but in comedy he seems to repose, or to luxuriate, as in a mode of thinking congenial to his nature. In his tragick scenes there is always something wanting, but his comedy often surpasses expectation or desire. His comedy pleases by the thoughts and the language, and his tragedy for the greater part by incident and action. His tragedy seems to be skill, his comedy to be instinct.

Shakespeare with his excellencies has likewise faults, and faults sufficient to obscure and overwhelm any other merit. I shall shew them in the proportion in which they appear to me, without envious malignity or superstitious veneration . . .

His first defect is that to which may be imputed most of the evil in books or in men. He sacrifices virtue to convenience, and is so much more careful to please than to instruct, that he seems to write without any moral purpose. From his writings indeed a system of social duty may be selected, for he that thinks reasonably must think morally; but his precepts and axioms drop casually from him; he makes no just distribution of good or evil, nor is always careful to shew in the virtuous a disapprobation of the wicked; he carries his persons indifferently through right and wrong, and at the close dismisses them without further care, and leaves their examples to operate by chance. This fault the barbarity of his age cannot extenuate; for it is always a writer's duty to make the world better, and justice is a virtue independant on time or place.

The plots are often so loosely formed, that a very slight consideration may improve them, and so carelessly pursued, that he seems not always fully to comprehend his own design. He omits opportunities of instructing or delighting, which the train of his story seems to force upon him, and apparently rejects those exhibitions which would be more affecting, for the sake of those which are more easy.

It may be observed, that in many of his plays the latter part is evidently neglected. When he found himself near the end of his work, and, in view of his reward, he shortened the labour, to snatch the profit . . .

He had no regard to distinction of time or place, but gives to one age or nation, without scruple, the customs, institutions, and opinions of another, at the expence not only of likelihood, but of possibility . . .

In his comick scenes he is seldom very successful, when he engages his characters in reciprocations of smartness and contests of sarcasm; their jests are commonly gross, and their pleasantry licentious; neither his gentlemen nor his ladies have much delicacy, nor are sufficiently distinguished from his clowns by any appearance of refined manners . . .

In tragedy his performance seems constantly to be worse, as his labour is more . . .

In narration he affects a disproportionate pomp of diction and a wearisome train of circumlocution, and tells the incident imperfectly in many words, which might have been more plainly deliverd in few . . .

His declamations or set speeches are commonly cold and weak, for his power was the power of nature . . .

It is incident to him to be now and then entangled with an unwieldy sentiment, which he cannot well express, and will not reject . . .

But the admirers of this great poet have most reason to complain when he approaches nearest to his highest excellence . . . What he does best, he soon ceases to do. He is not long soft and pathetick without some idle conceit, or contemptible equivocation . . .

A quibble is to *Shakespeare*, what luminous vapours are to the traveller; he follows it at all adventures, it is sure to lead him out of his way, and sure to engulf him in the mire. It has some malignant power over his mind, and its fascinations are irresistible. Whatever be the dignity or profundity of his disquisition, whether he be enlarging knowledge or exalting affection, whether he be amusing attention with incidents, or enchaining it in suspense, let but a quibble spring up before him, and he leaves his work unfinished. A quibble is the golden apple for which he will always turn aside from his career, or stoop from his elevation. A quibble, poor and barren as it is, gave him such delight, that he was content to purchase it, by the sacrifice of reason, propriety and truth. A quibble was to him the fatal *Cleopatra* for which he lost the world, and was content to lose it.

From the Preface to *The Plays of William Shakespeare*, 1765.

THOMAS WHATELY (–1772)

The writers upon dramatic composition have, for the most part, confined their observations to the fable; and the maxims received amongst them, for the conduct of it, are therefore emphatically called, *The Rules of the Drama*. It has been found easy to give and to apply them; they are obvious, they are certain, they are general: and poets without genius have, by observing them, pretended to fame; while critics without discernment have assumed importance from knowing them. But the regularity thereby established, though highly proper, is by no means the first requisite in a dramatic composition. Even waiving all consideration of those finer feelings which a poet's imagination or sensibility imparts, there is, within the colder provinces of judgment and of knowledge, a subject for criticism more worthy of attention than the common topics of discussion: I mean the distinction and preservation of *character*.[5]

From *Remarks on Some of the Characters of Shakespeare*, written c. 1770, published 1785.

MAURICE MORGANN (1726–1802)

The ideas which I have formed concerning the Courage and Military Character of the Dramatic Sir *John Falstaff* are so different from those which I find generally to prevail in the world, that I shall take the liberty of stating my sentiments on the subject; in hope that some per-

[5] In quoting this passage in his Introduction (xxxv–xxxvi) to *Eighteenth Century Essays on Shakespeare*, 1903, Professor D. Nichol Smith has described it as 'the first definite statement that the examination of Shakespeare's characters should be the main object of Shakesperian criticism'. Historically, Whately's *Remarks* pre-date William Richardson's strictly moral concern with Shakespeare's characters in his *Philosophical Analysis and Illustration of some of Shakespeare's Remarkable Characters*, 1774. (Ed.)

son, as unengaged as myself, will either correct or reform my error in this respect; or, joining himself to my opinion, redeem me from . . . the reproach of singularity.

I am to avow, then, that I do not clearly discern that Sir *John Falstaff* deserves to bear the character so generally given him of an absolute Coward; or, in other words, that I do not conceive *Shakespeare* ever meant to make Cowardice an essential part of his constitution . . .

It must, in the first place, be admitted that the appearances in this case are singularly strong and striking; and so they had need be, to become the ground of so general a censure. We see this extraordinary Character, almost in the first moment of our acquaintance with him, involved in circumstances of apparent dishonour; and we hear him familiarly called Coward by his most intimate companions . . . No wonder, therefore, that the word should go forth that *Falstaff* is exhibited as a character of Cowardice and dishonour.

What there is to the contrary of this, it is my business to discover. Much, I think, will presently appear; but it lies so dispersed, is so latent, and so purposely obscured, that the reader must have some patience whilst I collect it into one body, and make it the object of a steady and regular contemplation. . . . Perhaps, after all, the *real* character of *Falstaff* may be different from his *apparent* one; and possibly this difference between reality and appearance, whilst it accounts at once for our liking and our censure, may be the true point of humour in the character, and the source of all our laughter and delight. We may chance to find, if we will but examine a little into the nature of those circumstances which have accidentally involved him, that he was intended to be drawn as a character of much Natural courage and resolution; and be obliged thereupon to repeal those decisions which may have been made upon the credit of some general tho' unapplicable propositions; the common source of error in other and higher matters. A little reflection may perhaps bring us round again to the point of our departure, and unite our Understandings to our instinct.—Let us then for a moment *suspend* at least our decisions, and candidly and coolly inquire if Sir *John Falstaff* be, indeed, what he has so often been called by critic and commentator, male and female,—a *Constitutional Coward.*

It will scarcely be possible to consider the Courage of *Falstaff* as wholly detached from his other qualities: But I write not professedly of any part of his character, but what is included under the term, *Courage*; however, I may incidentally throw some lights on the whole. —The reader will not need to be told that this Inquiry will resolve itself of course into a Critique on the genius, the arts, and the conduct of *Shakespeare*: For what is *Falstaff*, what *Lear*, what *Hamlet*, or *Othello*, but different modifications of *Shakespeare's* thought? It is true that this Inquiry is narrowed almost to a single point: But general criticism is as uninstructive as it easy: *Shakespeare* deserves to be considered in detail; —a task hitherto unattempted.

c

With respect to every infirmity, except that of Cowardice, we must take him [Falstaff] as at the period in which he is represented to us. If we see him dissipated, fat,—it is enough;—we have nothing to do with his youth, when he might perhaps have been modest, chaste, *'and not an Eagle's talon in the waist'*. But *Constitutional Courage* extends to a man's whole life, makes a part of his nature, and is not to be taken up or deserted like a mere Moral quality. It is true, there is a Courage founded upon *principle*, or rather a principle independent of Courage, which will sometimes operate in spite of nature; a principle which prefers death to shame, but always refers itself, in conformity to its own nature, to the prevailing modes of honour, and the fashions of the age.—But Natural courage is another thing: It is independent of opinion; It adapts itself to occasions, preserves itself under every shape, and can avail itself of flight as well as of action.— . . . That Courage which is founded in nature and constitution, *Falstaff*, as I presume to say, possessed . . . The truth is that he had drollery enough to support himself in credit without the point of honour, and had address enough to make even the preservation of his life a point of drollery. The reader knows I allude, tho' something prematurely, to his fictitious death in the battle of Shrewsbury. This incident is generally construed to the disadvantage of *Falstaff*: It is a transaction which bears the external marks of Cowardice: It is also aggravated to the spectators by the idle tricks of the Player, who practises on this occasion all the attitudes and wild apprehensions of fear . . . There is no hint for this mummery in the Play: Whatever there may be of dishonour in *Falstaff's* conduct, he neither does or says any thing on this occasion which indicates terror or disorder of mind: On the contrary, this very act is a proof of his having all his wits about him . . .

Shakespeare is a name so interesting, that it is excusable to stop a moment, nay it would be indecent to pass him without the tribute of some admiration. He differs essentially from all other writers: Him we may profess rather to feel than to understand; and it is safer to say, on many occasions, that we are possessed by him, than that we possess him. And no wonder;—He scatters the seeds of things, the principles of character and action, with so cunning a hand, yet with so careless an air, and, master of our feelings, submits himself so little to our judgment, that every thing seems superior. We discern not his course, we see no connection of cause and effect, we are rapt in ignorant admiration, and claim no kindred with his abilities. All the incidents, all the parts, look like chance, whilst we feel and are sensible that the whole is design. His Characters not only act and speak in strict conformity to nature, but in strict relation to us; just so much is shewn as is requisite, just so much is impressed; he commands every passage to our heads and to our hearts, and moulds us as he pleases, and that with so much ease, that he never betrays his own exertions. We see these Characters act from the mingled motives of passion, reason, interest, habit, and complection

in all their proportions, when they are supposed to know it not themselves; and we are made to acknowledge that their actions and sentiments are, from those motives, the necessary result. He at once blends
and distinguishes every thing;—every thing is complicated, every thing
is plain . . . Or, is a character to be shewn in progressive change, and the
events of years comprized within the hour; with what a Magic hand
does he prepare and scatter his spells! . . . *Macbeth* changes under our
eye, *the milk of human kindness is converted to gall; he has supped full of
horrors,* and his *May of life is fallen into the sear, the yellow leaf* . . . On
such an occasion, a fellow, like *Rymer*, waking from his trance, shall
lift up his Constable's staff, and charge this great Magician, this daring
practicer of arts inhibited, in the name of *Aristotle,* to surrender; whilst
Aristotle himself, disowning his wretched Officer, would fall prostrate
at his feet and acknowledge his supremacy.—O supreme of Dramatic
excellence! (*might he say*) not to me be imputed the insolence of fools.
The bards of *Greece* were confined within the narrow circle of the
Chorus, and hence they found themselves constrained to practice, for
the most part, the precision, and copy the details of nature. I followed
them, and knew not that a larger circle might be drawn, and the Drama
extended to the whole reach of human genius. Convinced, I see that a
more compendious *nature* may be obtained; a nature of *effects* only, to
which neither the relations of place, or continuity of time, are always
essential. Nature, condescending to the faculties and apprehensions of
man, has drawn through human life a regular chain of visible causes and
effects: But Poetry delights in surprise, conceals her steps, seizes at once
upon the heart, and obtains the Sublime of things without betraying
the rounds of her ascent: True Poesy is *magic,* not *nature;* an effect
from causes hidden or unknown. To the Magician I prescribed no laws;
his law and his power are one; his power is his law. Him, who neither
imitates, nor is within the reach of imitation, no precedent can or ought
to bind, no limits to contain.

From *An Essay on the Dramatic Character of Sir John Falstaff,* 1777.

Critics on Shakespeare
1777-1904

CHARLES LAMB (1775-1834)

It may seem a paradox, but I cannot help being of opinion that the plays of Shakespeare are less calculated for performance on a stage, than those of almost any other dramatist whatever. Their distinguishing excellence is a reason that they should be so. There is so much in them, which comes not under the province of acting, with which eye, and tone, and gesture, have nothing to do.

. . . the practice of stage representation reduces everything to a controversy of elocution. Every character . . . must play the orator. The love-dialogues of Romeo and Juliet, those silver-sweet sounds of lovers' tongues by night; the more intimate and sacred sweetness of nuptial colloquy between an Othello or a Posthumus with their married wives, all those delicacies which are so delightful in the reading . . . by the inherent fault of stage representation, how are these things sullied and turned from their very nature by being exposed to a large assembly; when such speeches as Imogen addresses to her lord, come drawling out of the mouth of a hired actress, whose courtship, though nominally addressed to the personated Posthumus, is manifestly aimed at the spectators, who are to judge of her endearments and her returns of love . . .

The truth is, the Characters of Shakespeare are so much the objects of meditation rather than of interest or curiosity as to their actions, that while we are reading any of his great criminal characters,—Macbeth, Richard, even Iago,—we think not so much of the crimes which they commit, as of the ambition, the aspiring spirit, the intellectual activity, which prompts them to overleap those moral fences . . . But when we see these things represented, the acts which they do are comparatively every thing, their impulses nothing. The state of sublime emotion into which we are elevated by those images of night and horror which Macbeth is made to utter, that solemn prelude with which he entertains the time till the bell shall strike which is to call him to murder Duncan, —when we no longer read it in a book, when we have given up that vantage-ground of abstraction which reading possesses over seeing, and come to see a man in his bodily shape before our eyes actually preparing to commit a murder, if the acting be true and impressive . . . the painful anxiety about the act, the natural longing to prevent it while it yet seems unperpetrated, the too close pressing semblance of reality, give a pain and an uneasiness which totally destroy all the delight which the words in the book convey . . . The sublime images, the poetry alone, is that which is present to our minds in the reading . . .

. . . When we read the incantations of those terrible beings the Witches in *Macbeth*, though some of the ingredients of their hellish composition savour of the grotesque, yet is the effect upon us other than the most serious and appalling that can be imagined? Do we not feel spell-bound as Macbeth was? Can any mirth accompany a sense of their presence? We might as well laugh under a consciousness of the principle of Evil himself being truly and really present with us. But attempt to bring these beings on to a stage, and you turn them instantly into so many old women, that men and children are to laugh at. Contrary to the old saying, that 'seeing is believing', the sight actually destroys the faith . . .

Perhaps it would be no bad similitude, to liken the pleasure which we take in seeing one of these fine plays acted, compared with that quiet delight which we find in the reading of it, to the different feelings with which a reviewer, and a man that is not a reviewer, reads a fine poem. The accursed critical habit,—the being called upon to judge and pronounce, must make it quite a different thing to the former. In seeing these plays acted, we are affected just as judges. When Hamlet compares the two pictures of Gertrude's first and second husband, who wants to see the pictures? But in the acting, a miniature must be lugged out; which we know not to be the picture, but only to show how finely a miniature may be represented. The shewing of every thing, levels all things: it makes tricks, bows, and curtesies, of importance . . .

So to see Lear acted,—to see an old man tottering about the stage with a walking-stick, turned out of doors by his daughters in a rainy night, has nothing in it but what is painful and disgusting. We want to take him into shelter and relieve him. That is all the feeling which the acting of Lear ever produced in me. But the Lear of Shakespeare cannot be acted. The contemptible machinery by which they mimic the storm which he goes out in, is not more inadequate to represent the horrors of the real elements, than any actor can be to represent Lear . . . The greatness of Lear is not in corporal dimension, but in intellectual . . . On the stage we see nothing but corporal infirmities and weakness, the impotence of rage. While we read it, we see not Lear, but we are Lear: we are in his mind, we are sustained by a grandeur which baffles the malice of daughters and storms . . . [1]

From *On the Tragedies of Shakespeare, considered with reference to their fitness for Stage Representation*, 1811.

[1] Despite the gap of over thirty years between Morgann's Essay and Lamb's *On the Tragedies of Shakespeare*, there are close links in thought and attitude. Morgann's objection to the 'idle tricks of the Player' in accentuating Falstaff's apparent cowardice points forward, for example, to Lamb's more downright contention that Shakespeare is almost invariably distorted by stage representation. (Ed.)

SAMUEL TAYLOR COLERIDGE (1772-1834)

Shakespeare's characters, from Othello and Macbeth down to Dogberry
and the Grave-digger, may be termed ideal realities. They are not the
things themselves so much as abstracts of the things which a great
mind takes into itself and there naturalizes them to its own conception.
Take Dogberry: are no important truths there conveyed, no admirable
lessons taught, and no valuable allusions made to reigning follies,
which the poet saw must for ever reign? He is not the creature of the
day, to disappear with the day, but the representative and abstract of
truth which must ever be true, and of humour which must ever be
humorous . . .

In the plays of Shakespeare every man sees himself, without knowing
that he does so, as in some of the phenomena of nature, in the mist of
the mountain, the traveller beholds his own figure, but the glory round
the head distinguishes it from a mere vulgar copy. In traversing the
Brocken, in the north of Germany, at sunrise, the brilliant beams are
shot askance, and you see before you a being of gigantic proportions,
and of such elevated dignity that you only know it to be yourself by
similarity of action. In the same way, near Messina, natural forms, at
determined distances, are represented on an invisible mist, not as they
really exist, but dressed in all the prismatic colours of the imagination.
So in Shakespeare: every form is true, everything has reality for its
foundation; we can all recognize the truth, but we see it decorated with
such hues of beauty and magnified to such proportions of grandeur
that, while we know the figure, we know also how much it has been
refined and exalted by the poet.

If all that has been written upon Shakespeare by Englishmen were
burned, in the want of candles, merely to enable us to read one half of
what our dramatist produced, we should be great gainers.

It is a mistake to say that any of Shakespeare's characters strike us as
portraits; they have the union of reason perceiving, of judgement
recording, and of imagination diffusing over all a magic glory. While
the poet registers what is past, he projects the future in a wonderful
degree and makes us feel, however slightly, and see, however dimly,
that state of being in which there is neither past nor future but all is
permanent in the very energy of nature.

Although I have affirmed that all Shakespeare's characters are ideal,
and the result of his own meditation, yet a just separation may be made
of those in which the ideal is most prominent—where it is put
forward more intensely—where we are made more conscious of the
ideal, though in truth they possess no more nor less ideality; and of those
which, though equally idealized, the delusion upon the mind is of their
being real. The characters in the various plays may be separated into

those where the real is disguised in the ideal, and those where the ideal is concealed from us by the real. The difference is made by the different powers of mind employed by the poet in the representation . . .

From a report by J. P. Collier of a lecture by Coleridge, 1811–12.

Contrast the stage of the ancients with that of the time of Shakespeare, and we shall be struck with his genius: with them, it had the trappings of royal and religious ceremony; with him, it was a naked room, a blanket for a curtain; but with his vivid appeals the imagination figured it out,

A field for monarchs.

. . . He [Shakespeare] is not to be tried by ancient and classic rules, but by the standard of his age. That law of unity which has its foundation, not in factitious necessity of custom, but in nature herself, is instinctively observed by Shakespeare.

A *unity of feeling* pervades the whole of his plays. In *Romeo and Juliet* all is youth and spring—it is youth with its follies, its virtues, its precipitancies; it is spring with its odours, flowers, and transiency—the same feeling commences, goes through, and ends the play. The old men, the Capulets and Montagues, are not common old men; they have an eagerness, a hastiness, a precipitancy—the effect of spring. With Romeo his precipitate change of passion, his hasty marriage, and his rash death are all the effects of youth. With Juliet love has all that is tender and melancholy in the nightingale, all that is voluptuous in the rose, with whatever is sweet in the freshness of spring; but it ends with a long deep sigh, like the breeze of the evening. This unity of character pervades the whole of his dramas.

Of that species of writing termed *tragi-comedy*, too much has been produced, but it has been doomed to the shelf. With Shakespeare his comic constantly reacted on his tragic characters. Lear, wandering amidst the tempest, had all his feelings of distress increased by the overflowings of the wild wit of the Fool, as vinegar poured upon wounds exacerbates their pain; thus even his comic humour tends to the development of tragic passion.

The next character belonging to Shakespeare as Shakespeare was the *keeping at all times to the high road of life*. With him there were no innocent adulteries; he never rendered that amiable which religion and reason taught us to detest; he never clothed vice in the garb of virtue, like Beaumont and Fletcher . . . his fathers were roused by ingratitude, his husbands were stung by unfaithfulness; the affections were wounded in those points where all may and all must feel . . .

His dramas do not arise absolutely out of some one extraordinary circumstance; the scenes may stand independently of any such one connecting incident, as faithful reflections of men and manners. In his *mode of drawing characters* there were no pompous descriptions of a man by himself; his characters were to be drawn as in real life, from the whole course of the play, or out of the mouths of his enemies or friends.

This might be exemplified in the character of Polonius, which actors have often misrepresented. Shakespeare never intended to represent him as a buffoon. It was natural that Hamlet, a young man of genius and fire, detesting formality, and disliking Polonius for political reasons, as imagining that he had assisted his uncle in his usurpation, should express himself satirically; but Hamlet's words should not be taken as Shakespeare's conception of him. In Polonius a certain induration of character arose from long habits of business; but take his advice to Laertes, the reverence of his memory by Ophelia, and we shall find that he was a statesman of business, though somewhat past his faculties. One particular feature which belonged to his character was that his recollections of past life were of wisdom, and showed a knowledge of human nature, whilst what immediately passed before, and escaped from him, was emblematical of weakness.

From notes for a lecture on Shakespeare, 1813 (?)

Hamlet's character is the prevalence of the abstracting and generalizing habit over the practical. He does not want courage, skill, will or opportunity, but every incident sets him thinking; and it is curious and at the same time strictly natural that Hamlet, who all the play seems reason itself, should be impelled at last by mere accident to effect his object. I have a smack of Hamlet myself, if I may say so. . .

From Table Talk, 1827.

Lear is the most tremendous effort of Shakespeare as a poet; *Hamlet* as a philosopher or meditator; and *Othello* is the union of the two. There is something gigantic and unformed in the former two; but in the latter everything assumes its due place and proportion, and the whole mature powers of his mind are displayed in admirable equilibrium.

From Table Talk, 1822.

IAGO: Virtue! a fig! 'tis in ourselves that we are thus or thus.
Iago's passionless character, all *will* in intellect; therefore a bold partisan here of a truth, but yet of a truth converted into falsehood by absence of all the modifications which the frail nature of man would necessitate . . .

IAGO: Go to, farewell, put money enough in your purse;
   Thus do I ever make my fool my purse.
The triumph! Again, 'put money', after the effect has been fully produced. The last speech, Iago's soliloquy, shows the motive-hunting of motiveless malignity—how awful! In itself fiendish; while yet he was allowed to bear the divine image, it is too fiendish for his own steady view. He is a being next to devil, only *not* quite devil—and this Shakespeare has attempted—executed—without disgust, without scandal!

From some manuscript notes and marginalia on *Othello*, date uncertain.

Of all Shakespeare's plays *Macbeth* is the most rapid, *Hamlet* the slowest, in movement. *Lear* combines length with rapidity—like the hurricane and the whirlpool, absorbing while it advances . . .

It is well worthy of notice that *Lear* is the only serious performance of Shakespeare the interest and situations of which are derived from the assumption of a gross improbability, whereas Beaumont and Fletcher's tragedies are almost all founded on some out-of-the-way accident or exception to the general experience of mankind. But observe the matchless judgement of Shakespeare! First, improbable as the conduct of Lear is, in the first scene, yet it was an old story, rooted in the popular faith—a thing taken for granted already, and consequently without any of the *effects* of improbability. Secondly, it is merely the canvas to the characters and passions, a mere *occasion*—not (as in Beaumont and Fletcher) perpetually recurring as the cause and *sine qua non* of the incidents and emotions . . .

From some manuscript notes and marginalia on *King Lear.*

Shakespeare can be complimented only by comparison with himself: all other eulogies are either heterogeneous (e.g., in relation to Milton, Spenser, etc.) or flat truisms (e.g., to prefer him to Racine, Corneille, or even his own immediate successors, Fletcher, Massinger, etc.). The highest praise . . . of this play which I can offer in my own mind is the doubt which its perusal always occasions in me, whether it is not in all exhibitions of a giant power in its strength and vigour of maturity, a formidable rival of the *Macbeth, Lear, Othello* and *Hamlet. Feliciter audax* is the motto for its style comparatively with his other works, even as it is the general motto of all his works compared with those of other poets. Be it remembered, too, that this happy valiancy of style is but the representative and result of all the material excellencies so expressed.

. . . of all perhaps of Shakespeare's plays the most wonderful is the *Antony and Cleopatra*. There are scarcely any in which he has followed history more minutely, and yet few even of his own in which he impresses the notion of giant strength so much, perhaps none in which he impresses it more strongly. This is owing to the manner in which it is sustained throughout—that he *lives* in and through the play—to the numerous momentary flashes of nature counteracting the historic abstraction, in which take as a specimen the death of Cleopatra.

From undated notes on *Antony and Cleopatra.*

Measure for Measure is the single exception to the delightfulness of Shakespeare's plays. It is a hateful work, although Shakespearian throughout. Our feelings of justice are grossly wounded in Angelo's escape. Isabella herself contrives to be unamiable, and Claudio is detestable.

From Table Talk, 1827.

WILLIAM HAZLITT (1778–1830)

Shakespear has in this play shewn himself well versed in history and state-affairs. *Coriolanus* is a store-house of political commonplaces. Any one who studies it may save himself the trouble of reading Burke's Reflections or Paine's Rights of Man, or the Debates in both Houses of Parliament since the French Revolution or our own. The arguments for and against aristocracy or democracy, on the privileges of the few and the claims of the many, on liberty and slavery, power and the abuse of it, peace and war, are here very ably handled, with the spirit of a poet and the acuteness of a philosopher. Shakespear himself seems to have had a leaning to the arbitrary side of the question, perhaps from some feeling of contempt for his own origin; and to have spared no occasion of baiting the rabble. What he says of them is very true: what he says of their betters is also very true, though he dwells less upon it.—The cause of the people is indeed but little calculated as a subject for poetry . . . Poetry is right-royal. It puts the individual for the species, the one above the infinite many, might before right. A lion hunting a flock of sheep or a herd of wild asses is a more poetical subject than they; and we even take part with the lordly beast, because our vanity or some other feeling makes us disposed to place ourselves in the situation of the strongest party. So we feel some concern for the poor citizens of Rome when they meet together to compare their wants and grievances, till Coriolanus comes in and with blows and big words drives this set of 'poor rats', this rascal scum, to their homes and beggary before him. Their is nothing heroical in a multitude of miserable rogues not wishing to be starved, or complaining that they are like to be so: but when a single man comes forward to brave their cries and to make them submit to the last indignities, from mere pride and self-will, our admiration of his prowess is immediately converted into contempt for their pusillanimity. The insolence of power is stronger than the plea of necessity. The tame submission to usurped authority or even the natural resistance to it has nothing to excite or flatter the imagination: it is the assumption of a right to insult or oppress others that carries an imposing air of superiority with it. We had rather be the oppressor than the oppressed. The love of power in ourselves and the admiration of it in others are both natural to man: the one makes him a tyrant, the other a slave. Wrong dressed out in pride, pomp, and circumstance, has more attraction than abstract right.

The whole dramatic moral of *Coriolanus* is that those who have little shall have less, and that those who have much shall take all that others have left. The people are poor; therefore they ought to be starved. They are slaves; therefore they ought to be beaten. They work hard; therefore they ought to be treated like beasts of burden. They are ignorant; therefore they ought not to be allowed to feel that they want food, or clothing, or rest, that they are enslaved, oppressed, and miserable. This is the logic of the imagination and the passions; which seek to aggrandize what excites admiration and to heap contempt on misery, to raise power into tyranny, and to make tyranny absolute; to thrust down that which is low still lower, and to make wretches desperate: to exalt magistrates into kings, kings into gods; to degrade subjects to the rank of slaves, and slaves to the condition of brutes.

Dogberry and Verges in this play [*Much Ado About Nothing*] are inimitable specimens of quaint blundering and misprisions of meaning; and are a standing record of that formal gravity of pretension and total want common understanding, which Shakespear no doubt copied from real life, and which in the course of two hundred years appear to have ascended from the lowest to the highest offices in the state.

Henry V, it is true, was a hero, a king of England, and the conqueror of the king of France. Yet we feel little love or admiration for him. He was a hero, that is, he was ready to sacrifice his own life for the pleasure of destroying thousands of other lives: he was a king of England, but not a constitutional one, and we only like kings according to the law; lastly, he was a conqueror of the French king, and for this we dislike him less than if he had conquered the French people. How then do we like him? We like him in the play. There he is a very amiable monster, a very splendid pageant. As we like to gaze at a panther or a young lion in their cages in the Tower, and catch a pleasing horror from their glistening eyes, their velvet paws, and dreadless roar, so we take a very romantic, heroic, patriotic, and poetical delight in the boasts and feats of our younger Harry, as they appear on the stage and are confined to lines of ten syllables; where no blood follows the stroke that wounds our ears, where no harvest bends beneath horses' hoofs, no city flames, no little child is butchered, no dead men's bodies are found piled on heaps and festering the next morning—in the orchestra!

The character of Iago is one of the supererogations of Shakespear's genius. Some persons, more nice than wise, have thought this whole character unnatural, because his villainy is *without a sufficient motive*.[2] Shakespear, who was as good a philosopher as he was a poet, thought otherwise. He knew that the love of power, which is another name for the love of mischief, is natural to man. He would know this as well or better than if it had been demonstrated to him by a logical diagram, merely from seeing children paddle in the dirt or kill flies for sport. Iago in fact belongs to a class of character, common to Shakespear and at the same time peculiar to him; whose heads are as acute and active as their hearts are hard and callous. Iago is to be sure an extreme instance of the

[2] An allusion to Coleridge's view of Iago's 'motiveless malignity'. Coleridge and Hazlitt did not like one another. (Ed.)

kind; that is to say, of diseased intellectual activity, with the most perfect indifference to moral good or evil, or rather with a decided preference of the latter, because it falls more readily in with his favourite propensity, gives greater zest to his thoughts and scope to his actions. He is quite or nearly as indifferent to his own fate as to that of others; he runs all risks for a trifling and doubtful advantage, and is himself the dupe and victim of his ruling passion—an insatiable craving after action of the most difficult and dangerous kind. 'Our ancient' is a philosopher, who fancies that a lie that kills has more point in it than an alliteration or an antithesis; who thinks a fatal experiment on the peace of a family a better thing than watching the palpitations in the heart of a flea in a microscope; who plots the ruin of his friends as an exercise for his ingenuity, and stabs men in the dark to prevent *ennui*. His gaiety, such as it is, arises from the success of his treachery; his ease from the torture he has inflicted on others. He is an amateur of tragedy in real life; and instead of employing his invention on imaginary characters, or long-forgotten incidents, he takes the bolder and more desperate course of getting up his plot at home, casts the principal parts among his nearest friends and connections, and rehearses it in downright earnest, with steady nerves and unabated resolution.

It is the peculiar excellence of Shakespear's heroines, that they seem to exist only in their attachment to others. They are pure abstractions of the affections. We think as little of their persons as they do themselves, because we are let into the secrets of their hearts, which are more important. We are too much interested in their affairs to stop to look at their faces, except by stealth and at intervals. No one ever hit the true perfection of the female character, the sense of weakness leaning on the strength of its affections for support, so well as Shakespear—no one ever so well painted natural tenderness free from affectation and disguise —no one else ever so well shewed how delicacy and timidity, when driven to extremity, grow romantic and extravagant; for the romance of his heroines (in which they abound) is only an excess of the habitual prejudices of their sex, scrupulous of being false to their vows, truant to their affections, and taught by the force of feeling when to forgo the forms of propriety for the essence of it. His women were in this respect exquisite logicians; for there is nothing so logical as passion. They knew their own minds exactly; and only followed up a favourite purpose, which they had sworn to with their tongues, and which was engraven on their hearts, into its untoward consequences. They were the prettiest little set of martyrs and confessors on record.—Cibber, in speaking of the early English stage, accounts for the want of prominence and theatrical display in Shakespear's female characters from the circumstance, that women in those days were not allowed to play the parts of women, which made it necessary to keep them a good deal in the background. Does not this state of manners itself, which prevented their exhibiting themselves in public, and confined them to the relations and charities

of domestic life, afford a truer explanation of the matter? His women
are certainly very unlike stage-heroines; the reverse of tragedy-queens.
A selection from *Characters of Shakespear's Plays*, 1817.

JOHN KEATS (1795-1821)

I never quite despair and I read Shakespeare—indeed I shall I think
never read any other Book much . . . I am very near Agreeing with
Hazlit that Shakespeare is enough for us . . .

> From a letter to Benjamin Robert Haydon, Saturday & Sunday
> 10-11 May 1817. *The Letters of John Keats*, ed. Maurice Buxton
> Forman, 1931.

One of the three Books I have with me is Shakespear's Poems: I neer
found so many beauties in the Sonnets—they seem to be full of fine
things said unintentionally—in the intensity of working out conceits.
Is this to be borne? Hark ye!

> When lofty trees I see barren of leaves
>   Which erst from heat did canopy the herd,
> And Summer's green all girded up in sheaves,
>   Borne on the bier with white and bristly beard.

He has left nothing to say about nothing or anything . . .

> From a letter to John Hamilton Reynolds, Saturday 22 November
> 1817.

. . . it struck me, what quality went to form a Man of Achievement
especially in Literature, & which Shakespeare possessed so enormously
—I mean *Negative Capability*, that is when man is capable of being in
uncertainties, Mysteries, doubts, without any irritable reaching after
fact & reason—Coleridge, for instance, would let go by a fine isolated
verisimilitude caught from the Penetralium of mystery, from being
incapable of remaining content with half knowledge. This pursued
through Volumes would perhaps take us no further than this, that with
a great poet the sense of beauty overcomes every other consideration, or
rather obliterates all consideration.

> From a letter to George and Tom Keats, December 1817.

THOMAS DE QUINCEY (1785-1859)

All action in any direction is best expounded, measured, and made
apprehensible, by reaction. Now apply this to the case in *Macbeth*.
Here . . . the retiring of the human heart, and the entrance of the fiendish heart was to be expressed and made sensible. Another world has

stept in; and the murderers are taken out of the region of human things, human purposes, human desires. They are transfigured: Lady Macbeth is 'unsexed'; Macbeth has forgot that he was born of woman; both are conformed to the image of devils; and the world of devils is suddenly revealed. But how shall this be conveyed and made palpable? In order that a new world may step in, this world must for a time disappear. The murderers, and the murder must be insulated—cut off by an immeasurable gulf from the ordinary tide and succession of human affairs—locked up and sequestered in some deep recess; we must be made sensible that the world of ordinary life is suddenly arrested—laid asleep—tranced—racked into a dread armistice; time must be anni-hilated; relation to things without abolished; and all must pass self-withdrawn into a deep syncope and suspension of earthly passion. Hence it is, that when the deed is done, when the world of darkness is perfect, then the world of darkness passes away like a pageantry in the clouds: the knocking at the gate is heard; and it makes known audibly that the reaction has commenced; the human has made its reflux upon the fiendish; the pulses of life are beginning to beat again; and the re-establishment of the goings-on of the world in which we live, first makes us profoundly sensible of the awful parenthesis that had sus-pended them.

O mighty poet! Thy works are not as those of other men, simply and merely great works of art; but are also like the phenomena of nature, like the sun and the sea, the stars and the flowers; like frost and snow, rain and dew, hail-storm and thunder, which are to be studied with entire submission of our own faculties, and in the perfect faith that in them there can be no too much or too little, nothing useless or inert—but that, the farther we press in our discoveries, the more we shall see proofs of design and self-supporting arrangement where the careless eye had seen nothing but accident!

'On the Knocking at the Gate in *Macbeth*', *The London Magazine*, October 1823.

MATTHEW ARNOLD (1822–1888)

... the imitators of Shakespeare, fixing their attention on his wonderful gift of expression, have directed their imitation to this, neglecting his other excellences. These excellences, the fundamental excellences of poetical art, Shakespeare no doubt possessed them—possessed many of them in a splendid degree; but it may perhaps be doubted whether even he himself did not sometimes give scope to his faculty of expression to the prejudice of a higher poetical duty. For we must never forget that Shakespeare is the great poet he is from his skill in discerning and firmly conceiving an excellent action, from his power of intensely feeling a situation, of intimately associating himself with a character; not from his gift of expression, which rather even leads him astray, degenerating

sometimes into a fondness for curiosity of expression, into an irrita-
bility of fancy, which seems to make it impossible for him to say a thing
plainly, even when the press of the action demands the very directest
language, or its level character the very simplest. Mr Hallam . . . has had
the courage . . . to remark, how extremely and faultily difficult Shakespeare's language often is. It is so: you may find main scenes in some of
his greatest tragedies, *King Lear*, for instance, where the language is so
artificial, so curiously tortured, and so difficult, that every speech has to
be read two or three times before its meaning can be comprehended.
This over-curiousness of expression is indeed but the excessive employ-
ment of a wonderful gift—of the power of saying a thing in a happier
way than any other man; nevertheless, it is carried so far that one understands what M. Guizot meant, when he said that Shakespeare appears
in his language to have tried all styles except that of simplicity. He has
not the severe and scrupulous self-restraint of the ancients, partly no
doubt, because he had a far less cultivated and exacting audience: he has
indeed a far wider range than they had, a far richer fertility of thought;
in this respect he rises above them: in his strong conception of his subject,
in the genuine way in which he is penetrated with it, he resembles them,
and is unlike the moderns: but in the accurate limitation of it, the conscientious rejection of superfluities, the simple and rigorous development of it from the first line of his work to the last, he falls below them,
and comes nearer to the moderns. In his chief works, besides what he
has of his own, he has the elementary soundness of the ancients; he has
their important action and their large and broad manner: but he has not
their purity of method. He is therefore a less safe model; for what he
has of his own is personal, and inseparable from his own rich nature; it
may be imitated and exaggerated, it cannot be learned or applied as an
art; he is above all suggestive; more valuable, therefore, to young
writers as men than as artists. But clearness of arrangement, rigour of
development, simplicity of style—these may to a certain extent be
learned: and these may, I am convinced, be learned best from the
ancients, who although infinitely less suggestive than Shakespeare, are
thus, to the artist, more instructive.

From the Preface to A New Edition of *Poems by Matthew Arnold*,
1853.

EDWARD DOWDEN (1843–1913)

. . . it is certain that Shakspere's delight in human character, his quick
and penetrating sympathy with almost every variety of man, saved him
from any persistent injustice towards the world. But it can hardly be
doubted, that the creator of Hamlet, of Lear, of Timon, saw clearly, and
felt deeply, that there is a darker side to the world and to the soul of
man.
The Shakspere invariably bright, gentle, and genial is the Shakspere

of a myth. The man actually discoverable behind the plays was a man tempted to passionate extremes, but of strenuous will, and whose highest self pronounced in favour of sanity. Therefore he resolved that he would set to rights his material life, and he did so. And again he resolved that he would bring into harmony with the highest facts and laws of the world his spiritual being; and that in his own high fashion he accomplished also. The plays impress us as a long study of self-control,—of self-control at one with self-surrender to the highest facts and laws of human life. Shakspere set about attaining self-mastery, not of the petty, pedantic kind, which can be dictated by a director, or described in a manual, but large, powerful, luminous, and calm; and by sustained effort he succeeded in attaining this in the end. It is impossible to conceive that Shakspere should have traversed life, and felt its insufficiencies, and injuries, and griefs, without incurring Timon's temptation,—the temptation to fierce and barren resentment. What man or woman, who has sought good things, and with whom life has not gone altogether smoothly and pleasantly, has not known, if not for days and weeks then for hours, if not for hours then for intense moments, a Timon within him, incapable for the while of making any compromise with the world, and fiercely abandoning it with cries of weak and passionate revolt? And when again such a man accepts life, and human society, it is not what it had been before. The music of his life is a little lowered throughout; the pegs are set down. Or what had been a nerve is changed to a sinew. Or he finds himself a little more indifferent to pain. Or now and then a pungent sentence escapes his lips, which is unintelligible to those who had only known his former self.

In the character of Timon, Shakspere gained dramatic remoteness from his own personality. It would have been contrary to the whole habit of the dramatist's genius to have used one of his characters merely as a mask to conceal his visage, while he relieved himself with lyrical vehemence of the feelings that oppressed him. No: Shakspere, when Timon was written, had attained self-possession, and could transfer himself with real disinterestedness into the person of the young Athenian favourite of fortune. This, in more than one instance, was Shakspere's method,—having discovered some single point of sympathy between his chief character and his past or present self, to secure freedom from all mere lyrical intensity by studying that one common element under conditions remote from those which had ever been proper or peculiar to himself.

From *Shakspere, His Mind and Art*, 1874.

First Period.—Returning now from our more detailed classification, let us glance once more at the four periods into which we divided Shakspere's career of authorship. The first, which I named *In the workshop*, was the period during which Shakspere was learning his trade as a dramatic craftsman. Starting at the age of twenty-four or twenty-six, he made rapid progress, and cannot but have been aware of this. The works of Shakspere's youth—experiments in various directions—are all marked by the presence of vivacity, cleverness, delight in beauty, and a quick enjoyment of existence. If an industrious apprentice, he was also a gay and courageous one.

Second Period.—As yet, however, he wrote with small experience of human life; the early plays are slight or fanciful, rather than real and massive. But now Shakspere's imagination began to lay hold of real life; he came to understand the world and the men in it; his plays begin to deal in an original and powerful way with the matter of history . . . During this period Shakspere's work grows strong and robust. It was the time when he was making rapid advance in worldly prosperity, and accumulating the fortune on which he meant to retire as a country gentleman. I name the second period therefore *In the world.*

Third Period.—Before it closed Shakspere had known sorrow: his son was dead; his father died probably soon after Shakspere had written his *Twelfth Night*; his friend of the *Sonnets* had done him wrong. Whatever the cause may have been, the fact seems certain that the poet now ceased to care for tales of mirth and love, for the stir and movement of history, for the pomp of war; he needed to sound, with his imagination, the depths of the human heart; to inquire into the darkest and saddest parts of human life; to study the great mystery of evil. The belief in human virtue, indeed, never deserts him: in *Lear* there is a Cordelia; in *Macbeth*, a Banquo; even Troilus will be the better, not the worse, for his disenchantment with Cressida; and it is because Timon would fain love that he is driven to hate. Still, during this period, Shakspere's genius left the bright surface of the world, and was at work in the very heart and centre of things. I have named it *Out of the Depths.*

Fourth Period.—The tragic gloom and suffering were not, however, to last for ever. The dark cloud lightens and rolls away, and the sky appears purer and tenderer than ever. The impression left upon the reader by Shakspere's last plays is that, whatever his trials and sorrows and errors may have been, he had come forth from them wise, large-hearted, calm-souled. He seems to have learned the secret of life, and while taking his share in it, to be yet disengaged from it; he looks down upon life, its joys, its griefs, its errors, with a grave tenderness, which is almost pity. The spirit of these last plays is that of serenity which results from fortitude, and the recognition of human frailty; all of them express a deep sense of the need of repentance and the loveliness of youthful joy, such as one feels who looks on these things without possessing or any longer desiring to possess them. Shakspere in this period is most like his own Prospero. In these 'Romances' and in the 'Fragments', a super-natural element is present; man does not strive with circumstance and with his own passions in darkness; the gods preside over our human lives and fortunes, they communicate with us by vision, by oracles, through the elemental powers of nature. Shakspere's faith seems to have been that there is something without and around our human lives, of which we know little, yet which we know to be beneficient and divine. And it will be felt that the name which I have given to this last period— Shakspere having ascended out of the turmoil and trouble of action, out of the darkness and tragic mystery, the places haunted by terror and crime, and by love contending with these, to a pure and serene elevation—it will be felt that the name, *On the heights,* is neither inappropriate nor fanciful.

From *Shakspere,* Literature Primer, 1877.

RICHARD G. MOULTON (1849–1924)

Amongst ordinary readers of Shakespeare, Character-Interest, which is largely independent of performance, has swallowed up all other interests; and most of the effects which depend upon the connection and relative force of incidents, and on the compression of the details into a given space, have been completely lost. Shakespeare is popularly regarded as supreme in the painting of human nature, but careless in the construction of Plot: and worst of all, Plot itself, which it has been the mission of the English Drama to elevate into the position of the most intellectual of all elements in literary effect, has become degraded in conception to the level of a mere juggler's mystery. It must then be laid down distinctly at the outset of the present enquiry that the Drama is to be considered throughout relatively to its acting . . . The interpretation of a character must include what an actor can put into it; in dealing with effects regard must be had to surroundings which a reader might easily overlook, but which would be present to the eye of a spectator; and no conception of the movement of a drama will be adequate which has not appreciated the rapid sequence of incidents that crowds the crisis of a life-time or a national revolution into two or three hours of actual time. The relation of Drama to its acting will be exactly similar to that of Music to its performance, the two being perfectly separable in their exposition, but never disunited in idea.

From *Shakespeare As a Dramatic Artist,* 1885.

G. B. SHAW (1856–1950)

What a pity it is that the people who love the sound of Shakespear so seldom go on the stage! The ear is the sure clue to him: only a musician can understand the play of feeling which is the real rarity in his early plays. In a deaf nation these plays would have died long ago. The moral attitude in them is conventional and secondhand: the borrowed ideas, however finely expressed, have not the over-powering human interest of those original criticisms of life which supply the rhetorical element in his later works. Even the individualization which produces the old-established British speciality, the Shakespearian 'delineation of character', owes all its magic to the turn of the line, which lets you into the secret of its utterer's mood and temperament, not by its commonplace meaning, but by some subtle exaltation, or stultification, or slyness, or delicacy, or hesitancy, or whatnot in the sound of it. In short, it is the score and not the libretto that keeps the work alive and fresh; and this is why only musical critics should be allowed to meddle with Shakespear—especially early Shakespear.

From 'Poor Shakespear!', *The Saturday Review*, 2 February 1895.

. . . One can hardly forgive Shakespear quite for the worldly phase in which he tried to thrust such a Jingo hero as his Harry V down our throats. The combination of conventional propriety and brute masterfulness in his public capacity with a low-lived blackguardism in his private tastes is not a pleasant one. No doubt he is true to nature as a picture of what is by no means uncommon in English society, an able young Philistine inheriting high position and authority, which he holds on to and goes through with by keeping a tight grip on his conventional and legal advantages . . . His popularity . . . is like that of a prizefighter: nobody feels for him as for Romeo or Hamlet. Hotspur, too, though he is stimulating as ginger cordial is stimulating, is hardly better than his horse; and King Bolingbroke, preoccupied with his crown exactly as a miser is preoccupied with his money, is equally useless as a refuge for our affections, which are thus thrown back undivided on Falstaff, the most human person in the play, but none the less a besotted and disgusting old wretch. And there is neither any subtlety nor (for Shakespear) much poetry in the presentation of all these characters. They are labelled and described and insisted upon with the roughest directness . . . Fortunately, they offer capital opportunities for interesting acting. Bolingbroke's long discourse to his son on the means by which he struck the imagination and enlisted the snobbery of the English people gives the actor a chance comparable to the crafty early scenes in Richelieu. Prince Hal's humor is seasoned with sportsmanlike cruelty and the insolence of conscious mastery and contempt to the point of occasionally making one shudder. Hotspur is full of energy; and Falstaff is, of course, an unrivalled part for the right sort of comedian. Well acted, then, the play is a good one in spite of there not being a single tear in it. Ill acted—O heavens!

From 'Henry IV', *The Saturday Review*, 16 May 1896.

The world being yet little better than a mischievous schoolboy, I am afraid it cannot be denied that Punch and Judy holds the field still as the most popular of dramatic entertainments. And of all its versions . . . Shakespear's Richard III is the best. It has abundant devilry, humor, and character, presented with luxuriant energy of diction in the simplest form of blank verse . . . Richard is the prince of Punches: he delights Man by provoking God, and dies unrepentant and game to the last. His incongruous conventional appendages, such as the Punch hump, the conscience, the fear of ghosts, all impart a spice of outrageousness which leaves nothing lacking to the fun of the entertainment, except the solemnity of those spectators who feel bound to take the affair as a profound and subtle historic study.

From 'Richard Himself Again', *The Saturday Review*, 26 December 1896.

The popularity of Rosalind [in *As You Like It*] is due to three main causes. First, she only speaks blank verse for a few minutes. Second, she only wears a skirt for a few minutes . . . Third, she makes love to the man instead of waiting for the man to make love to her—a piece of natural history which has kept Shakespear's heroines alive, whilst generations of properly governessed young ladies, taught to say 'No' three times at least, have miserably perished.

From 'Toujours Shakespear', *The Saturday Review*, 5 December 1896.

Shakespear's Antony and Cleopatra must needs be as intolerable to the true Puritan as it is vaguely distressing to the ordinary healthy citizen, because, after giving a faithful picture of the soldier broken down by debauchery, and the typical wanton in whose arms such men perish, Shakespear finally strains all his huge command of rhetoric and stage pathos to give a theatrical sublimity to the wretched end of the business, and to persuade foolish spectators that the world was well lost by the twain.

From 'Better than Shakespear?', Preface to *Three Plays for Puritans*, 1900.

Shakespear is for an afternoon, but not for all time.

From 'The Immortal William', *The Saturday Review*, 2 May 1896.

A. C. BRADLEY (1851–1935)

A Shakespearean tragedy as so far considered may be called a story of exceptional calamity leading to the death of a man of high estate. But it is clearly much more than this, and we have now to regard it from another side. No amount of calamity which merely befell a man, descending from the clouds like lightning, or stealing from the darkness like pestilence, could alone provide the substance of its story . . . The calamities of tragedy do not simply happen, nor are they sent; they proceed mainly from actions, and those the actions of men.

We see a number of human beings placed in certain circumstances;

and we see, arising from the co-operation of their characters in these circumstances, certain actions. These actions beget others, and these others beget others again, until this series of inter-connected deeds leads by an apparently inevitable sequence to a catastrophe. The effect of such a series on imagination is to make us regard the sufferings which accompany it, and the catastrophe in which it ends, not only or chiefly as something which happens to the persons concerned, but equally as something which is caused by them . . .

The 'story' or 'action' of a Shakespearean tragedy does not consist, of course, solely of human actions or deeds; but the deeds are the predominant factor. And these deeds are, for the most part, actions in the full sense of the word; not things done ' 'tween sleep and wake', but acts or omissions thoroughly expressive of the doer,—characteristic deeds. The centre of the tragedy, therefore, may be said with equal truth to lie in action issuing in character, or in character issuing in action.

Shakespeare's main interest lay here. To say that it lay in *mere* character, or was a pyschological interest, would be a great mistake, for he was dramatic to the tips of his fingers. It is possible to find places where he has given a certain indulgence to his love of poetry, and even to his turn for general reflections; but it would be very difficult, and in his later tragedies perhaps impossible, to detect passages where he has allowed much such freedom to the interest in character apart from action. But for the opposite extreme, for the abstraction of mere 'plot' (which is a very different thing from the tragic 'action'), . . . it is clear that he cared even less. I do not mean that this interest is absent from his dramas; but it is subordinate to others, and is so interwoven with them that we are rarely conscious of it apart . . . What we do feel strongly, as a tragedy advances to its close, is that the calamities and catastrophe follow inevitably from the deeds of men, and that the main source of these deeds is character. The dictum that, with Shakespeare, 'character is destiny' is no doubt an exaggeration, and one that may mislead (for many of his tragic personages, if they had not met with peculiar circumstances, would have escaped a tragic end, and might even have lived fairly untroubled lives); but it is the exaggeration of a vital truth.

From *Shakespearean Tragedy*, Lecture I, 1904.

Critics on Shakespeare since 1904

WALTER RALEIGH (1861–1922)

No dramatist can create live characters save by bequeathing the best of himself to the children of his art, scattering among them a largess of his own qualities, giving, it may be, to one his wit, to another his philosophic doubt, to another his love of action, to another the simplicity and constancy that he finds deep in his own nature. There is no thrill of feeling communicated from the printed page but has first been alive in the mind of the author; there was nothing alive in his mind that was not intensely and sincerely felt. Plays like those of Shakespeare cannot be written in cold blood; they call forth the man's whole energies, and take toll of the last farthing of his wealth of sympathy and experience. In the plays we may learn what are the questions that interest Shakespeare most profoundly and recur to his mind with most insistence; we may note how he handles his story, what he rejects, and what he alters, changing its purport and fashion; how many points he is content to leave dark; what matters he chooses to decorate with the highest resources of his romantic art, and what he gives over to be the sport of triumphant ridicule; how in every type of character he emphasizes what most appeals to his instinct and imagination, so that we see the meaning of character more plainly than it is to be seen in life . . .

From *Shakespeare*, Chapter I, 1907.

GEORGE SAINTSBURY (1845–1933)

But it is quite certain that anyone who, with fair education and competent wits, gives his days and nights to the reading of the actual plays will be a far better judge than anyone who allows himself to be distracted by comment and controversy. The important thing is to get the Shakespearean atmosphere, to feel the breath of the Shakespearean spirit. And it is doubtful whether it is not much safer to get this first, and at first hand, than to run the risk of not getting it while investigating the exact meaning of every allusion and the possible date of every item. The more thoroughly and impartially this spirit is observed and extracted, the more will it be found to consist in the subjection of all things to what may be called the romantic process of presenting them in an atmosphere of poetical suggestion rather than as sharply defined and logically stated. But this romantic process is itself characterized and pervaded by a philosophical depth and width of conception of life which is not usually associated with romance. And it is enlivened and made actual by the dramatic form which, whether by separable or inseparable accident, the writer has adopted . . .

From 'Shakespeare: Life and Plays', *The Cambridge History of English Literature*, V, Chapter 8, 1910.

T. S. ELIOT (1888–1965)

Few critics have ever admitted that *Hamlet* the play is the primary problem, and Hamlet the character only secondary. And Hamlet the character has had an especial temptation for that most dangerous type of critic: the critic with a mind which is naturally of the creative order, but which through some weakness in creative power exercises itself in criticism instead. These minds often find in Hamlet a vicarious existence for their own artistic realization. Such a mind had Goethe, who made of Hamlet a Werther; and such had Coleridge, who made of Hamlet a Coleridge; and probably neither of these men in writing about Hamlet remembered that his first business was to study a work of art. The kind of criticism that Goethe and Coleridge produced, in writing of Hamlet, is the most misleading kind possible. For they both possessed un-questionable critical insight, and both make their critical aberrations the more plausible by the substitution—of their own Hamlet for Shakespeare's—which their creative gift effects. We should be thankful that Walter Pater did not fix his attention to this play.

Two writers of our time, Mr J. M. Robertson and Professor Stoll of the University of Minnesota, have issued small books which can be praised for moving in the other direction. Mr Stoll performs a service in recalling to our attention the labours of the critics of the seventeenth and eighteenth centuries, observing that

'they knew less about psychology than more recent Hamlet critics, but they were nearer in spirit to Shakespeare's art; and as they insisted on the importance of the effect of the whole rather than on the importance of the leading character, they were nearer, in their old-fashioned way, to the secret of dramatic art in general.'

Qua work of art, the work of art cannot be interpreted; there is nothing to interpret; we can only criticize it according to standards, in comparison to other works of art; and for 'interpretation' the chief task is the presentation of relevant historical facts which the reader is not assumed to know. Mr Robertson points out, very pertinently, how critics have failed in their 'interpretation' of *Hamlet* by ignoring what ought to be very obvious: that *Hamlet* is a stratification, that it represents the efforts of a series of men, each making what he could out of the work of his predecessors. The *Hamlet* of Shakespeare will appear to us very differently if, instead of treating the whole action of the play as due to Shakespeare's design, we perceive his *Hamlet* to be superimposed upon much cruder material which persists even in the final form.

. . . The upshot of Mr Robertson's examination is, we believe, irrefragable: that Shakespeare's *Hamlet*, so far as it is Shakespeare's, is a play dealing with the effect of a mother's guilt upon her son, and that Shakespeare was unable to impose this motive successfully upon the 'intractable' material of the old play.

Of the intractability there can be no doubt. So far from being Shakespeare's masterpiece, the play is most certainly an artistic failure. In several ways the play is puzzling, and disquieting as is none of the others. Of all the plays it is the longest and is possibly the one on which Shakespeare spent most pains; and yet he has left in it superfluous and inconsistent scenes which even hasty revision should have noticed. The versification is variable. Lines like

Look, the morn, in russet mantle clad,
Walks o'er the dew of yon high eastern hill,

are of the Shakespeare of *Romeo and Juliet*. The lines in Act V. Sc. ii,

Sir, in my heart there was a kind of fighting
That would not let me sleep . . .

are of his quite mature. Both workmanship and thought are in an unstable position. We are surely justified in attributing the play, with that other profoundly intesting play of 'intractable' material and astonishing versification, *Measure for Measure*, to a period of crisis, after which follow the tragic successes which culminate in *Coriolanus*. *Coriolanus* may not be as 'interesting' as *Hamlet*, but it is, with *Antony and Cleopatra*, Shakespeare's most assured artistic success. And probably more people have thought *Hamlet* a work of art because they found it interesting, than have found it interesting because it is a work of art. It is the 'Mona Lisa' of literature.

The grounds of *Hamlet's* failure are not immediately obvious. Mr Robertson is undoubtedly correct in concluding that the essential emotion of the play is the feeling of a son towards a guilty mother . . .

This, however, is by no means the whole story. It is not merely the 'guilt of a mother' that cannot be handled as Shakespeare handled the suspicion of Othello, the infatuation of Antony, or the pride of Coriolanus . . . *Hamlet*, like the sonnets, is full of some stuff that the writer could not drag to light, contemplate, or manipulate into art. And when we search for this feeling, we find it, as in the sonnets, very difficult to localize. You cannot point to it in the speeches; indeed, if you examine the two famous soliloquies you see the versification of Shakespeare, but a content which might be claimed by another, perhaps by the author of the *Revenge of Bussy d'Ambois*, Act V. Sc. i. We find Shakespeare's

Hamlet not in the action, not in any quotations that we might select, so much as in an unmistakable tone which is unmistakably not in the earlier play.

The only way of expressing emotion in the form of art is by finding an 'objective correlative'; in other words, a set of objects, a situation, a chain of events which shall be the formula of that *particular* emotion; such that when the external facts, which must terminate in sensory experience, are given, the emotion is immediately evoked. If you examine any of Shakespeare's more successful tragedies, you will find this exact equivalence; you will find that the state of mind of Lady Macbeth walking in her sleep has been communicated to you by a skilful accumulation of imagined sensory impressions; the words of Macbeth on hearing of his wife's death strike us as if, given the sequence of events, these words were automatically released by the last event in the series. The artistic 'inevitability' lies in this complete adequacy of the external to the emotion; and this is precisely what is deficient in *Hamlet*. Hamlet (the man) is dominated by an emotion which is inexpressible, because it is in *excess* of the facts as they appear. And the supposed identity of Hamlet with his author is genuine to this point: that Hamlet's bafflement at the absence of objective equivalent to his feelings is a prolongation of the bafflement of his creator in the face of his artistic problem. Hamlet is up against the difficulty that his disgust is occasioned by his mother, but that his mother is not an adequate equivalent for it; his disgust envelops and exceeds her. It is thus a feeling which he cannot understand; he cannot objectify it, and it therefore remains to poison life and obstruct action. None of the possible actions can satisfy it; and nothing that Shakespeare can do with the plot can express Hamlet for him. And it must be noticed that the very nature of the *données* of the problem precludes objective equivalence. To have heightened the criminality of Gertrude would have been to provide the formula for a totally different emotion in Hamlet; it is just *because* her character is so negative and insignificant that she arouses in Hamlet the feeling which she is incapable of representing.

The 'madness' of Hamlet lay to Shakespeare's hand; in the earlier play a simple ruse, and to the end, we may presume, understood as a ruse by the audience. For Shakespeare it is less than madness and more than feigned. The levity of Hamlet, his repetition of phrase, his puns, are not part of a deliberate plan of dissimulation, but a form of emotional relief. In the character Hamlet it is the buffoonery of an emotion which can find no outlet in action; in the dramatist it is the buffoonery of an emotion which he cannot express in art. The intense feeling, ecstatic or terrible, without an object or exceeding its object, is something which every person of sensibility has known; it is doubtless a subject of study for pathologists. It often occurs in adolescence: the ordinary person puts these feelings to sleep, or trims down his feelings to fit the business world; the artist keeps them alive by his ability to intensify the world to his emotions. The Hamlet of Laforgue is an adolescent; the Hamlet of Shakespeare is not, he has not that explanation and excuse. We must simply admit that here Shakespeare tackled a problem which proved too much for him. Why he attempted it at all is an insoluble puzzle; under compulsion of what experience he attempted to express the inexpressibly horrible, we cannot ever know. We need a great many facts in his biography; and we should like to know whether, and when, and after or at the same time as what personal experience, he read Montaigne, II, xii, *Apologie de Raimond Sebond*. We should have, finally, to know something which is by hypothesis unknowable, for we assume it to be an experience which, in the manner indicated, exceeded the facts. We should have to understand things which Shakespeare did not understand himself.

From 'Essay on *Hamlet*', 1919.

E. E. STOLL (1874–1959)

So far are Shakespeare's other heroes removed from the infection that they are, all of them, great of heart, bold in deed, even strong and lithe of limb, as today no hero need be. They are worthies, champions . . . Othello, as he bids his uncle let him come forth, cries, 'I have made my way through more than twenty times your stop'; old Lear, in his last hours, kills Cordelia's executioner; Macbeth, Antony and Coriolanus perform prodigies of valour single-handed in the field. And just such, we have seen, is Hamlet . . . Indeed, the dramatist seems to have deliberately suppressed or avoided much of what might remind us of the student or scholar. . . No one calls him a scholar save Ophelia, who at the same time calls him a courtier and soldier; and no one scorns him or condescends to him . . . as a bookish, dreamy, impractical person . . . He is a student of the Renaissance, taking to his sword as readily as to his book,—indeed in all Shakespeare who takes to his sword more readily? . . .

Now Shakespeare is, in his method, emphatic and unmistakable; and if he had suddenly resolved to abandon heroic romance, and undertake a novel—a psychological—type of character, such as Hamlet has, in the last century, been understood to be, he would have tried to make him as different as possible from his other characters—make him really a Werther, an Aprile, or, say, a Romeo who kept his sword like a dancer and shunned danger and death. Instead, he has, save for the delay, given him all the stout qualities of the others. Instead, he has kept for him all the stout qualities he had had in Kyd. How, then, could an audience detect the difference, if a difference there was meant to be? And to indicate a difference that the audience could not detect, Shakespeare, of course, was not the man to have lifted a finger. He was not painting pictures that were never to be seen, not shooting arrows into the air. He was writing plays which plain and common people were expected to like, and in order to like them, of course, must understand.

How naturally—and how differently from us—they understood the play now in question we have learned already.

From *Hamlet: An Historical and Comparative Study*, 1919.

HARLEY GRANVILLE-BARKER (1877–1946)

'Lear is essentially impossible to be represented on a stage'—and later critics have been mostly of Charles Lamb's opinion. My chief business in this Preface will be to justify, if I can, its title there.

Shakespeare meant it to be acted, and he was a very practical playwright. So that should count for something. Acted it was, and with success enough for it to be presented before the king at Whitehall . . . And Burbage's performance of King Lear remained a vivid memory. At the Restoration it was one of the nine plays selected by Davenant for his theatre. He had in mind, doubtless, its 'reforming and making fit'—all of them except *Hamlet* and *Othello* were to suffer heavily from that. But Downes, his prompter, tells us that it was '. . . *Acted* exactly as Mr *Shakespear* wrote it . . .'—several times apparently—before Nahum Tate produced his version in 1681. This hotchpotch held the stage for the next hundred and fifty years and more, though from Garrick's time onwards it would generally be somewhat re-Shakespeareanized. One cannot prove Shakespearean stage-worthiness by citing Tate, but how far is it not Tate rather than Shakespeare that Lamb condemns? He has Shakespeare's play in mind, but he had never seen it acted . . . And he never considers Shakespeare's play in relation to Shakespeare's stage . . . The orotund acting of his day, its conventional tricks, can have been but a continual offence to his sensitive ear and nicety of taste. He here takes his revenge—and it is an ample one—for many evenings of such suffering. He never stopped to consider whether there might not be more even to the actor's despised art than that.

A profounder and a more searching indictment of the play's stage-worthiness comes from A. C. Bradley in the (for me) most remarkable of those remarkable lectures on Shakespearean Tragedy. To him it seems '. . . Shakespeare's greatest achievement, but . . . *not* his best play'. The entire argument should be read; but this, I think, sums it up not unfairly. He says that 'The stage is the test of strictly dramatic quality, and *King Lear* is too huge for the stage . . . It has scenes immensely effective in the theatre . . . But (not to speak of defects due to mere carelessness) that which makes the *peculiar* greatness of *King Lear*,— the immense scope of the work; the mass and variety of intense experience which it contains; the interpenetration of sublime imagination, piercing pathos, and humour almost as moving as the pathos; the vastness of the convulsion both of nature and of human passion; the vagueness of the scene where the action takes place, and of the movements of the figures which cross this scene; the strange atmosphere, cold and dark, which strikes on us as we enter this scene, enfolding those figures and magnifying their dim outlines like a winter mist; the half-realized suggestions of vast universal powers working in the world of individual fears and passions, all this interferes with dramatic clearness even when the play is read, and in the theatre not only refuses to reveal itself fully through the sense but seems to be almost in contradiction with their reports.' And later: 'The temptation of Othello and the scene of Duncan's murder may lose upon the stage, but they do not lose their *essence*, and they gain as well as lose. The Storm-scenes in *King Lear* gain nothing, and their very *essence* is destroyed.' For this essence is poetry, and, he concludes, '. . . such poetry as cannot be transferred to the space behind the foot-lights, but has its being only in imagination. Here then is Shakespeare at his very greatest, but not the mere dramatist Shakespeare.'

Notice, first of all, how widely Bradley's standpoint is removed from that—we may venture to surmise it—of 'the mere dramatist Shakespeare' and his fellows the actors. To say of certain scenes that they were 'immensely effective in the theatre' and add that they *lost* there 'very little of the spell they have for imagination', to argue that 'the temptation of Othello and the scene of Duncan's murder may lose upon the stage, but they do not lose their *essence*, and they gain as well as lose'—it would have sounded to them queer commendation. For in whatever Shakespeare wrote was the implied promise that in the theatre it would *gain*. Bradley passes easily to: 'The Storm-scenes in *King Lear* gain nothing, and their very *essence* is destroyed.' But the dramatist, on his defence, would rightly refuse to follow him; for the premises to the argument are not the same.

Bradley and Lamb may be right in their conclusions. It is possible that this most practical and loyal of dramatists did for once—despite himself, driven to it by his unpremeditating genius—break his promise and betray his trust by presenting to his fellows a play, the capital parts of which they simply could not act. Happily for them, they and their audiences never found him out. But if Bradley is right, not the most perfect performance can be a fulfilment, can be aught but a betrayal of *King Lear*. There is the issue. The thing is, of course, incapable of proof. The best that imperfect human actors can give must come short of perfection, and the critic can always retort to their best that his imagination betters it. Bradley's argument is weighty. Yet—with all deference to a creat critic—I protest that, as it stands, it is not valid. He is contending that a practical and practised dramatist has here written a largely impracticable play. Before condemning these 'Storm-scenes' he should surely consider their stagecraft—their mere stagecraft. For may not 'the mere dramatist' have his answer hidden there? But this—starting from his standpoint of imaginative reader—he quite neglects to do.

From *Prefaces to Shakespeare, 2, King Lear, Antony and Cleopatra*, 1930. (Opening remarks on *King Lear*.)

. . . It is always instructive to watch Shakespeare getting his play with its crew under way, to see him stating his subjects, setting his characters in opposition. Some lead off, fully themselves from the start, some seem to hang on his hands, saying what they have to say in sound conventional phrase, some he may leave all but mute, uncertain yet, it would seem, of his own use for them. Not till the whole organism has gathered strength and abounds in a life of its own is the true mastery to be seen. Even so, in *King Lear* there is more to be accounted for. In no other of the plays, I think, unless it be *Macbeth*, are we so conscious of the force of an emotion overriding, often, a character's self-expression, and of a vision of things to which the action itself is but a foreground. And how this and the rest of the play's individuality is made manifest by the form as well as the substance of the dialogue, by the shaping and colour of its verse and prose, it is, of course, of primary importance for producer and actors to observe. There is no one correct way of speaking Shakespeare's verse and prose, for he had no one way of writing it. One way grew out of another with him. Little of the method of *Romeo and Juliet* will be left in *King Lear*, much of the method of *Hamlet* still may be. But the fresh matter of a play will provoke a fresh manner, and its interpretation must be as freshly approached.

   Ibid. (Remarks on *The Method of the Dialogue* in *King Lear*.)

We should never, probably, think of Shakespeare as sitting down to construct a play as an architect must design a house, in the three dimensions of its building. His theatre did not call for this, as the more rigorous economics of modern staging may be said to do. He was liker to a musician, master of an instrument, who takes a theme and, by generally recognized rules, improvises on it; or even to an orator, so accomplished that he can carry a complex subject through a two-hour speech, split it up, run it by divers channels, digress, but never for too long, and at last bring the streams abreast again to blend them in his peroration. Clarity of statement, a sense of proportion, of the value of contrast, justness of emphasis—in these lie the technique involved; and these, it will be found, are the dominant qualities of Shakespeare's stage-craft—of the craft merely, be it understood.

   He is apt to lay the main lines of his story very firmly and simply, and to let us see where we are going from the start, to cut the complexities from borrowed plots, and if any side issue later promises distraction, to make (literally) short work of it. Here he reduces the actual story to simplicity itself. Antony breaks from Cleopatra to patch up an insincere peace with Caesar, since Pompey threatens them both; he marries Octavia, and deserts her to return to Cleopatra; war breaks out, Caesar defeats them and they kill themselves. That is the plot; every character is concerned with it, hardly a line is spoken that does not relate to it; and much strength lies in this concentration of interest. There is no under-plot, nor any such obvious relief (which must, however, bring dissipation of interest too) as Falstaff, Nym, Bardolph, Pistol and Fluellen give to the heroics of the Henriad.

But, for a broad picturesque contrast, Roman and Egyptian are set against each other; and this opposition braces the whole body of the play, even as conflict between character and character will sustain each scene. He asserts the contrast at once; for we assemble expectant in a theatre, therefore first impressions cut deep and a first stretch of action will be of prime importance. We have two indignant, hard-bitten Roman campaigners, who must stand aside while the procession passes—
Cleopatra, her ladies, the train, with Eunuchs fanning her.—and see Antony in the toils. Their bitter comments follow it. Next, we have a taste of the chattering, shiftless, sensual, credulous Court, with its trulls and wizards and effeminates. Then we see Antony, with Rome, the 'garboils' of his wife's making and the threats of Pompey calling him, breaking his toils for a time; and the statement of the theme is complete.

Ibid. (Remarks on *The Play's Construction* in relation to *Antony and Cleopatra*.)

G. WILSON KNIGHT (1897–   )

At the start, I would draw a distinction between the terms 'criticism' and 'interpretation' . . . 'Criticism' to me suggests a certain process of deliberately objectifying the work under consideration; the comparison of it with other similar works in order especially to show in what respects it surpasses, or falls short of, those works; the dividing its 'good' from its 'bad'; and, finally, a formal judgement as to its lasting validity. 'Interpretation', on the contrary, tends to merge into the work it analyses: it attempts, as far as possible, to understand its subject in the light of its own nature . . .; it avoids discussion of merits, and, since its existence depends entirely on its original acceptance of the validity of the poetic unit which it claims, in some measure, to translate into discursive reasoning, it can recognize no division of 'good' from 'bad' . . . Criticism is a judgement of vision; interpretation a reconstruction of vision. In practice, it is probable that neither can exist . . . quite divorced from the other. The greater part of poetic commentary pursues a middle course between criticism and interpretation. But sometimes work is created of so resplendent a quality, so massive a solidity of imagination, that adverse criticism beats against it idly as the wind that flings its ineffectual force against a mountain-rock. Any profitable commentary on such work must necessarily tend towards a pure interpretation.

The work of Shakespeare is of this transcendent order . . . But today there is a strong tendency to 'criticize' Shakespeare, to select certain aspects of his mature works and point out faults . . . Now it will generally be found that when a play is understood in its totality, these faults automatically vanish . . . In reading, watching, or acting Shakespeare for pure enjoyment we accept everything. But when we think 'critically' we see faults which are not implicit in the play nor our enjoyment of it, but merely figments of our own minds. We should not, in fact, think critically at all: we should interpret our original imaginative experience into the slower consciousness of logic and intellect, preserving something of that child-like faith which we possess, or should possess, in the theatre. It is exactly this translation from one order of consciousness to another that interpretation claims to perform. Uncritically, and passively, it receives the whole of the poet's vision; it then proceeds to re-express this experience in its own terms.

To receive this whole Shakespearian vision within the intellectual consciousness demands a certain and very definite act of mind. One must be prepared to see the whole play in space as well as in time . . . A Shakespearian tragedy is set spatially as well as temporally in the mind. By this I mean that there are throughout the play a set of correspondences which relate to each other independently of the time-sequence which is the story: such are the intuition-intelligence opposition active within and across *Troilus and Cressida*, the death-theme in *Hamlet*, the nightmare evil of *Macbeth*. This I have sometimes called the play's 'atmosphere'. In interpretation of *Othello* it has to take the form of an essential relation, abstracted from the story, existing between the Othello, Desdemona, and Iago conceptions. Generally, however, there is unity, not diversity. Perhaps it is what Aristotle meant by 'unity of idea'. Now if we are prepared to see the whole play laid out, so to speak, as an area, being simultaneously aware of these thickly-scattered correspondences in a single view of the whole, we possess the unique quality of the play in a new sense. 'Faults' begin to vanish into thin air. Immediately we begin to realize necessity where before we saw irrelevance and beauty dethroning ugliness. For the Shakespearian person is intimately fused with this atmospheric quality; he obeys a spatial as well as a temporal necessity. Gloucester's mock-suicide, Malcolm's detailed confession of crimes, Ulysses' long speech on order, are cases in point. But because we, in our own lives and those of our friends, see events most strongly as a time-sequence—thereby blurring our vision of other significances—we next, quite arbitrarily and unjustly, abstract from the Shakespearian drama that element which the intellect most easily assimilates; and, finding it not to correspond with our own life as we see it, begin to observe 'faults'. This, however, is apparent only after we try to rationalize our impressions; what I have called the 'spatial' approach is implicit in our imaginative pleasure to a greater or less degree always. It is, probably, the ability to see larger and still larger areas of a great work spatially with a continual widening of vision that causes us to appreciate it more deeply, to own it with our minds more surely, on every reading; whereas at first, knowing it only as a story, much of it may have seemed sterile, and much of it irrelevant.

And finally, as to 'character'. In the following essays the term is refused, since it is so constantly entwined with a false and unduly ethical criticism. So often we hear that 'in *Timon of Athens* it was Shakespeare's intention to show how a generous but weak character may come to ruin through an unwise use of his wealth'; that 'Shakespeare wished in *Macbeth* to show how crime inevitably brings retribution'; that, 'in *Antony and Cleopatra* Shakespeare has given us a lesson concerning the dangers of an uncontrolled passion'. These are purely imaginary examples, coloured for my purpose, to indicate the type of ethical criticism to which I refer. It continually brings in the intention-concept, which our moral-philosophy, rightly or wrongly, involves. Hence, too, the constant and fruitless search for 'motives' sufficient to account for Macbeth's and Iago's actions: since the moral critic feels he cannot blame a 'character' until he understands his 'intentions', and without the opportunity of praising and blaming he is dumb. It is not, clearly, possible to avoid ethical considerations; nor is it desirable . . . but we should follow our dramatic intuitions. A person in the drama may act in such a way that we are in no sense antagonized but are aware of beauty and supreme interest only; yet the analogy to that same action may well be intolerable to us in actual life. When such a divergence occurs the commentator must be true to his artistic, not his normal, ethic. Large quantities of Shakespeare criticism have wrecked themselves on the teeth of this dualism . . . ethical terms, though they must frequently occur in interpretation, must only be allowed in so far as they are used in absolute obedience to the dramatic and aesthetic significance: in which case they cease to be ethical in the usual sense.

This false criticism is implied by the very use of the word 'character'. It is impossible to use the term without any tinge of a morality which blurs vision. The term, which in ordinary speech often denotes the degree of moral control exercised by the individual over his instinctive passions, is altogether unsuited to those persons of poetic drama whose life consists largely of passion unveiled. *Macbeth* and *King Lear* are created in a soul-dimension of primal feeling, of which in real life we may be only partly conscious or may be urged to control by a sense of right and wrong. In fact, it may well seem that the more we tend away from the passionate and curbless life of poetic drama, the stronger we shall be as 'characters'. And yet, in reading *Macbeth* or *King Lear* we are aware of strength, not weakness . . . We must observe, then, this paradox: the strong protagonist of poetic drama would probably appear a weakling if he were a real man; and, indeed, the critic who notes primarily Macbeth's weakness is criticizing him as a man rather than a dramatic person.

. . . we should regard each play as a visionary whole, close-knit in person-ification, atmospheric suggestion, and direct poetic-symbolism: three modes of transmission, equal in their importance . . . Each incident, each turn of thought, each suggestive symbol throughout *Macbeth* or *King Lear* radiates inwards from the play's circumference to the burning central core without knowledge of which we shall miss their relevance

E

and necessity . . . The persons of Shakespeare have been analysed carefully in point of psychological realism, yet in giving so detailed and prolix a care to any one element of the poet's expression, the commentator, starting indeed from a point on the circumference, instead of working into the heart of the play, pursues a tangential course, riding, as it were, on his own life-experiences farther and farther from his proper goal. Such is the criticism that finds fault with the Duke's decisions at the close of *Measure for Measure*: if we are to understand the persons of Shakespeare we should consider always what they do rather than what they might have done. Each person, event, scene, is integral to the poetic statement: the removing, or blurring, of a single stone in the mosaic will clearly lessen our chance of visualizing the whole design . . .

Nor will a sound knowledge of the stage and the especial theatrical technique of Shakespeare's work render up its imaginative secret. True, the plays were written as plays, and meant to be acted. But that tells us nothing relevant to our purpose. It explains why certain things cannot be found in Shakespeare: it does not explain why the finest things, the fascination of *Hamlet*, the rich music of *Othello*, the gripping evil of *Macbeth*, the pathos of *King Lear*, and the gigantic architecture of *Timon of Athens* came to birth.

From Chapter I ('On the Principles of Shakespeare Interpretation') of *The Wheel of Fire*, 1930 (revised and enlarged, 1949).

L. C. KNIGHTS (1906–   )

The inquiry involves an examination of certain critical presuppositions, and of these the most fruitful of irrelevancies is the assumption that Shakespeare was pre-eminently a great 'creator of characters'. So extensive was his knowledge of the human heart (so runs the popular opinion) that he was able to project himself into the minds of an infinite variety of men and women and present them 'real as life' before us. Of course he was a great poet as well, but the poetry is an added grace which gives to the atmosphere of the plays a touch of 'magic' and which provides us with the thrill of single memorable lines and lyric passages . . .

There is no need to search for examples in the field of Shakespeare criticism . . . The most illustrious example is, of course, Dr Bradley's *Shakespearean Tragedy* . . . It is assumed throughout the book that the most profitable dicussion of Shakespeare's tragedies is in terms of the characters of which they are composed—'The centre of the tragedy may be said with equal truth to lie in action issuing from character, or in character issuing in action . . . What we feel strongly, as a tragedy advances to its close, is that the calamities and catastrophe follow inevitably from the deeds of men, and that the main source of these deeds is character. The dictum that, with Shakespeare, "character is destiny"

is no doubt an exaggeration . . . but it is the exaggeration of a vital truth.'
It is this which leads Dr Bradley to ask us to imagine Posthumus in
the place of Othello, Othello in the place of Posthumus, and to conjec-
ture upon Hamlet's whereabouts at the time of his father's death.

The influence of the assumption is pervasive. Not only are all the
books of Shakespeare criticism (with a very few exceptions) based upon
it, it invades scholarship (the notes to the indispensable Arden edition
may be called in evidence), and in school children are taught to think
they have 'appreciated' the poet if they are able to talk about the
characters—aided no doubt by the neat summaries provided by Mr
Verity which they learn so assiduously before examinations.

In the mass of Shakespeare criticism there is not a hint that
'character'—like 'plot', 'rhythm', 'construction' and all our other
critical counters—is merely an abstraction from the total response in the
mind of the reader or spectator, brought into being by written or spoken
words; that the critic therefore—however far he may ultimately range—
begins with the words of which a play is composed . . .

A Shakespeare play is a dramatic poem. It uses action, gesture,
formal grouping and symbols, and it relies upon the general conventions
governing Elizabethan plays. But, we cannot too often remind ourselves,
its end is to communicate a rich and controlled experience by means of
words—words used in a way to which, without some training, we are
no longer accustomed to respond. To stress in the conventional way
character or plot, or any of the other abstractions that can be made, is
to impoverish the total response. 'It is in the total situation rather than
in the wrigglings of individual emotion that the tragedy lies.'[1]

We should not look for perfect verisimilitude to life [says Mr Wilson
Knight] but rather see each play as an expanded metaphor, by means of
which the original vision has been projected into forms roughly corres-
pondent with actuality, conforming thereto with greater or less exacti-
tude according to the demands of its nature . . . The persons, ultimately,
are not human at all, but purely symbols of a poetic vision.[2]

It would be easy to demonstrate that this approach is essential even
when dealing with plays like *Hamlet* or *Macbeth* which can be made to
yield something very impressive in the way of 'character'. And it is the
only approach which will enable us to say anything at all relevant about
plays like *Measure for Measure* or *Troilus and Cressida* which have con-
sistently baffled the critics.

The habit of regarding Shakespeare's persons as 'friends for life' or,
maybe, 'deceased acquaintances', is responsible for most of the vagaries
that serve as Shakespeare criticism. It accounts for the artificial simpli-
fications of the editors . . . It accounts for the 'double time' theory for
Othello. It accounts for Dr Bradley's Notes. It is responsible for all the
irrelevant moral and realistic canons that have been applied to Shakes-

[1] M. C. Bradbrook, *Elizabethan Stage Conditions*, p. 102.
[2] G. Wilson Knight, *The Wheel of Fire*, p. 16.

E*

peare's plays, for the sentimentalizing of his heroes (Coleridge and Goethe on Hamlet) and his heroines. And the loss is incalculable. Losing sight of the *whole* dramatic pattern of each play, we inhibit the development of that full complex response that makes our experience of a Shakespeare play so very much more than an appreciation of 'character'—that is, usually, of somebody else's 'character'. That more complete, more intimate possession can only be obtained by treating Shakespeare primarily as a poet.

From 'How Many Children Had Lady Macbeth?', *An Essay in the Theory and Practice of Shakespeare Criticism*, 1933, Part One.

Since everyone who has written about Shakespeare probably imagines that he has 'treated him primarily as a poet', some explanation is called for. How should we read Shakespeare?

We start with so many lines of verse on a printed page which we read as we should read any other poem. We have to elucidate the meaning . . . and to unravel ambiguities; we have to estimate the kind and quality of the imagery and determine the precise degree of evocation of particular figures; we have to allow full weight to each word, exploring its 'tentacular roots', and to determine how it controls and is controlled by the rhythmic movement of the passage in which it occurs. In short, we have to decide exactly why the lines 'are so and not otherwise'.

As we read other factors come into play. The lines have a cumulative effect. 'Plot', aspects of 'character', and recurrent 'themes'—all 'precipitates from the memory'—help to determine our reaction at a given point. There is a constant reference backwards and forwards. But the work of detailed analysis continues to the last line of the last act. If the razor-edge of sensibility is blunted at any point we cannot claim to have read what Shakespeare wrote, however often our eyes may have travelled over the page. A play of Shakespeare's is a precise particular experience, a poem—and precision and particularity are exactly what is lacking in the greater part of Shakespeare criticism, criticism that deals with *Hamlet* or *Othello* in terms of abstractions that have nothing to do with the unique arrangement of words that constitutes these plays.

Ibid., Part Two.

CAROLINE F. E. SPURGEON (1869–1942)

I embarked on this task of collecting and classifying the images, because it seemed to me that it might provide a new method of approach to Shakespeare, and I believe I have, by a happy fortune, hit on such a method, hitherto untried, which is yielding most interesting and important results. It not only throws light from a fresh angle, as we have seen in the tragedies, upon Shakespeare's imaginative and pictorial vision, upon his own ideas about his own plays and the characters in them, but it seems to me to serve as an absolute beacon in the skies with regard to the vexed question of authorship. It also enables us to get nearer to Shakespeare himself, to his mind, his tastes, his experiences, and his deeper thought than does any other single way I know of studying him.

I believe that a poet, and more especially a dramatic poet, to some extent unconsciously 'gives himself away' in his images. He may be, and in Shakespeare's case is, almost entirely objective in his dramatic characters and their views and opinions, yet, like the man who under stress of emotion will show no sign of it in eye or face, but will reveal it in some muscular tension, the poet unwittingly reveals his own innermost likes and dislikes, observations and interests, associations of thought, attitudes of mind and beliefs, in and through the images, the verbal pictures he draws to illuminate something quite different in the speech and thought of his characters.

. . . I believe that when these pictures are all assembled, and can be studied in proportion, it is possible to build up from them a fairly trustworthy picture, not only of the peculiarities of his bodily senses and organism, of his tastes and interests, of things seen and deeply felt, especially in youth, but also to some extent a picture of his attitude of mind, his opinions and beliefs such as you could never gain with any certainty from opinions or beliefs expressed directly as such by any one of his characters. I can, perhaps, illustrate by two or three examples how this seems to me to work.

When Othello brings out the horror of the contrast between the fair looks of Desdemona and what he believes her deeds entirely by means of *smell*, lamenting

O thou weed,
Who art so lovely fair and smell'st so sweet
That the sense aches at thee, would thou hadst ne'er been born!

and answering her piteous query, 'Alas, what ignorant sin have I committed?' with the agonized cry

What committed!
Heaven stops the nose at it;

we not only realize Othello's torture, racked between love and repulsion, but we also know incidentally that Shakespeare had a sensitive nose.

And when in addition we find that he repeatedly expresses disgust and loathing through the medium of revolting smells, chiefly of unwashed humanity and decaying substances, and that to his imagination sin and evil deeds always *smell foully*, we are justified in assuming that he himself intensely disliked bad smells.

From 'Shakespeare's Iterative Imagery', lecture delivered and published in 1931.

By far the clearest and most striking example that I have met with of this tendency to group repeatedly a certain chain of ideas round some particular emotional or mental stimulus, is another group of ideas centring round an animal. This is so marked in its repetition that it has been noted by others—I mean the dog, licking, candy, melting group, called up inevitably by the thought of false friends or flatterers.

It is quite certain that one of the things which rouses Shakespeare's bitterest and deepest indignation is feigned love and affection assumed for a selfish end. He who values so intensely—above all else in human life—devoted and disinterested love, turns almost sick when he watches flatterers and sycophants bowing and cringing to the rich and powerful purely in order to get something out of them for themselves. It is as certain as anything can be, short of direct proof, that he had been hurt, directly or indirectly, in this particular way. No one who reads his words carefully can doubt that he had either watched someone, whose friendship he prized, being deceived by fawning flatterers, or that he himself had suffered from a false friend or friends who, for their own ends, had drawn out his love while remaining 'themselves as stone'.

From *Shakespeare's Imagery and What It Tells Us*, 1935, Chapter 10.

W. H. CLEMEN (1909–   )

Caroline F. Spurgeon deserves the credit of having classified and investigated the whole treasury of Shakespeare's images in a systematic manner for the first time. And here, for the first time, is shown for almost all the plays, how in the imagery of a drama *leitmotive* appear which are closely related to the play's theme and atmosphere. In the first part of her book, Miss Spurgeon introduces the reader to the subject matter of the images with the aim of approaching Shakespeare's personality in this way. She evaluates the images as documentations of Shakespeare's senses, tastes and interests, and also as witnesses to his personal equipment, his bodily and mental qualities. Miss Spurgeon holds that the fact that Shakespeare preferred certain groups and classes of images reveals his own sympathies and dislikes. His imagery is thus taken to be a transcript of his own personal world, a mirror of his own individual outlook on things. The conception underlying the following study differs from this view. It seems evident that Shakespeare's choice of an image or simile at a given moment in the play is determined far more by the dramatic issues arising out of that moment than by his individual sympathies.

From *The Development of Shakespeare's Imagery*, Chapter 2, 1951 (a translation of *Shakespeare's Bilder*, 1936).

The imagery in *Coriolanus*, compared with that in *Macbeth* or *Antony and Cleopatra*, is less intricate and complex . . . The images are mostly clear, short, obvious, and illustrate a plain theme. This definiteness and simplicity of imagery corresponds to the play's mood. The warlike atmosphere, the vigorous and active mind of Coriolanus, the speed of the action, the absence of meditative or sentimental scenes, all these combine to call forth brevity and clarity of diction,—a 'Roman distinctness' determines plot and style. Moreover, the play involves a sharp and clearly marked contrast that could well be brought out by the imagery.

The function of the imagery to emphasize and repeat the play's main theme is particularly interesting in *Coriolanus*. For here the imagery throws much light on Shakespeare's attitude towards a general problem, to which he gave dramatic life. We cannot draw deductions and inferences from every play of Shakespeare's as to his own attitude towards certain problems. He even seems to conceal what he himself thinks of his characters. This is, of course, betrayed to us by the play taken as a whole; it is seldom explicitly said in this or that passage. But while Shakespeare rarely expresses his opinions in his plays, he frequently implies very subtly his attitude towards certain problems. And imagery is one of the subtlest and most effective methods he employs for this purpose.

The contrast between the commanding figure of Coriolanus and the baseness of the 'rabble' is vividly brought out by a series of images which, at the same time, reveal Shakespeare's intense dislike of the masses, of the never-to-be-trusted rabble . . .

Our unconscious imagination is . . . influenced by the numerous short metaphors and nouns characterizing the rabble. These epithets may be found on almost every page. Taken as a whole, they represent the most intense characterization by means of imagery ever attempted by Shakespeare.

Of animal names applied to the rabble we have *dogs, cats, curs, hares, geese, camels, mules, crows, minnows, goats*. All these animals (some of them occurring repeatedly) are represented as cowardly creatures which are to be hunted, which know nothing but their greedy feeding . . .

Shakespeare must have been particularly struck by the greediness of the rabble, as this feature is repeatedly emphasized . . . The rabble, unless kept in awe by the senate, would, in Coriolanus' phrase, 'feed on one another' (I.i.192), their 'affections are a sick man's appetite' (I.i.182).

We now turn from these images of disdain and disgust to their antithesis, namely those describing Coriolanus. It is Shakespeare's admiration for great and heroic men that leads him to characterize them by means of images of boldness and force. Their impressive and victorious appearance on the stage is re-echoed and enhanced in imagery. Antony, Caesar, Othello are examples of this art of characterization, Antony being the most forceful. Coriolanus is another important example. In contrast with the timorous and insignificant animals which characterize the common people we find brave and noble animals as symbols of the heroic nature of Coriolanus. He is a dragon (IV.i.30; IV.vii.23; V.iv.12), an eagle (V.vi.115), a steed (I.ix.12) and a tiger (V.iv.32). Volumnia compares him to the bear from which enemies flee like children (I.iii.34), and Aufidius likens him to the osprey who takes the fish 'by sovereignty of nature' (by *fish* Rome is meant) (IV.vii.35). There are other images which embody the irresistible, victorious and at the same time terrible character of his warlike nature . . . On the other hand, Shakespeare counterbalances these grandiose images by another type of imagery which, through ironical exaggeration, suggests a more critical point of view. It is Menenius who characterizes Coriolanus in the following words: When he walks, he moves like an engine, and the ground shrinks before his treading: he is able to pierce a corslet with his eye; talks like a knell, and his hum is a battery. He sits in his state, as a thing made for Alexander . . . He wants nothing of a god but eternity and a heaven to throne in. (V.iv.19).

. . . In this play Shakespeare indeed realized what one of the tribunes bitterly remarked: 'All tongues speak of him' (II.i.221). Coriolanus is present in every scene, his personality is reflected in almost every utterance of the other characters.

The technique of characterizing the hero by means of images used by other characters began with the repulsive animal-images which surround the figure of Richard III; but as early as *Richard II* we can discern how the range of these images has widened. Certain comparisons, however, appear again and again and may be traced throughout all the histories: the symbol of the sun or of the star for the king; plant-imagery or the image of the ship for human existence. In *Antony and Cleopatra* the images of light, and the cosmic-imagery characterizing Antony, are linked up with the symbols accompanying the common catastrophe. Thus *Antony and Cleopatra* marks a climax in the combined use of characterizing and symbolic imagery; but *Coriolanus* represents an achievement in another respect. For in no other play did Shakespeare honour his hero with such a wealth of imagery. The omnipresence of Coriolanus produces one of the most powerful dramatic effects of this play.

Such omnipresence of the hero in a Shakespearian drama cannot be demonstrated simply by listing all the passages referring to the hero. Such an enumeration must remain more or less of an approximation; by this method we can at most divine something of that which will always be a secret.

Condensed and abridged version of *The Development of Shakespeare's Imagery*, Chapter 15.

J. DOVER WILSON (1881–   )

It is in *Hamlet* that the two critics [Professor Clemen and Miss Spurgeon] draw closest together and where, if anywhere, the later book is indebted to the earlier. Yet one could not find a better illustration

of their difference in outlook and approach than here. Pointing out the
dominant part played in *Hamlet* by images of disease and corruption,
Professor Spurgeon relates this first to the state of Denmark, to the
mental condition of its Prince, and by inference to the mood of the
dramtist. Shakespeare, she concludes, sees the problem of *Hamlet*

> 'not as the problem of an individual at all, but as something greater
> and even more mysterious, as a condition for which the individual
> himself is apparently not responsible any more than the sick man is
> to blame for the infection which strikes and devours him, but which
> nevertheless, in its course and development, impartially and re-
> lentlessly, annihilates him and others, innocent and guilty alike. That
> is the tragedy *Hamlet*, as it is perhaps the chief mystery of life.'[3]

Behind this pronouncement looms an image of the philosophic Shakespeare, brooding upon life at the threshold of the Tragic Period which
Dowden labelled 'The Depths' in 1875. In other words, it expresses
the emotional reaction of the nineteenth-century school of Shakespearian criticism. Turn to the chapter on *Hamlet* [in Professor Clemen's
book] and you will find much that is highly suggestive about particular
aesthetic matters, including the light which the hero's choice of images
throws upon his character, but nothing at all about 'the problem of
Hamlet'. As for the images of corruption, which Professor Clemen
agrees contribute greatly to the general atmosphere of the play, these
are related not to the character of *Hamlet*, still less to the mood of his
creator, but to the dramaturgy which gave the play its artistic unity,
springing as they do from two fundamental 'facts' of the plot: the
filthy incestuous crime of Gertrude which infects the mind of her son,
and the 'leperous distilment' by which Claudius had infected the body
of his sleeping brother,

> Most lazar-like, with vile and loathsome crust.

From the Preface to the English edition of *Shakespeare's Bilder*, 1951'

We are driven . . . to conclude with Loening, Bradley, Clutton-Brock
and other critics that Shakespeare meant us to imagine Hamlet suffering
from some kind of mental disorder throughout the play. Directly,
however, such critics begin trying to define the exact nature of the
disorder, they go astray. Its immediate origin cannot be questioned; it
is caused . . . by the burden which fate lays upon his shoulders. We are
not, however, at liberty to go outside the frame of the play and seek
remoter origins in his past history. It is now well known, for instance,
that a breakdown like Hamlet's is often due to seeds of disturbance
planted in infancy and brought to evil fruition under the influence of
mental strain of some kind in later life. Had Shakespeare been com-
posing *Hamlet* to-day, he might conceivably have given us a hint of such
an infantile complex. But he knew nothing of these matters and to

[3] *Shakespeare's Imagery and What It Tells Us*, p. 319.

write as if he did is to beat the air. We may go further. It is entirely misleading to attempt to describe Hamlet's state of mind in terms of modern psychology at all, not merely because Shakespeare did not think in these terms, but because . . . Hamlet is a character in a play, not in history. He is part only, if the most important part, of an artistic master-piece, of what is perhaps the most successful piece of dramatic illusion the world has ever known. And at no point of the composition is the illusion more masterly contrived than in this matter of his distraction.[4]

From *What Happens in Hamlet*, 1935, Chapter 6.

Traditional Shakespearian criticism from Coleridge to Bradley has been almost entirely concerned with the tragedies. Nothing is more curious, for example, than the treatment meted out to the comedies in that representative and very influential Victorian critique, Dowden's *Shakespeare: his Mind and Art* (1875). In Chapter 2, which gives a general survey of the plays as a whole, we have, as a matter of form, references to the comedies, while they are spoken of again in a later chapter on 'The Humour of Shakespeare'. But . . . from beginning to end of the book he . . . has nothing to tell us about the general qualities of his comedies, and deals so slightly with the greatest of them all, *Twelfth Night*, that its name is not even to be found in his index. And yet, as his title shows, he claimed to be enlightening the world on the principles of Shakespeare's art. Clearly it was the tragedies which chiefly interested him.

This concentration upon the tragedies to the neglect of the comedies has had two unfortunate results. First of all, it has, despite Dowden, given us a false idea of Shakespeare's spiritual and artistic development. We look at him far too much through the tragic end of the telescope and so have belittled him. And in the second place, it has impaired our vision of the tragedies themselves . . . The stuff of his 'mind and art' was first woven on the comic loom and it retained something of this comic texture right up to the end. Imagine *Hamlet* without Polonius or without the Prince's antic disposition; *Lear* without the Fool; *Macbeth* without the Porter (which Coleridge, insensitive to comedy, declared could not be Shakespeare's!), and the truth of this is obvious.

---

[4] This passage written in the nineteen-thirties anticipates the kind of objections to be raised against the psychological speculations concerning Hamlet's mental disorder in *Hamlet and Oedipus*, 1949. Dr Ernest Jones writes for instance: 'How if, in fact, Hamlet had in years gone by, as a child, bitterly resented having had to share his mother's affection even with his own father, had regarded him as a rival, and had secretly wished him out of the way . . . ? The actual realization of his early wish in the death of his father at the hands of a jealous rival would then have stimulated into activity these "repressed" memories, which would have produced, in the form of depression and other suffering, and obscure aftermath of his childhood's conflict.' But, as Professor Dover Wilson had pointed out years before, 'Hamlet is a character in a play, not in history' (or in some psychological case-book). (Ed.)

On the other hand, he carried the tragic baton in his knapsack from the outset of his career. As we shall note, nearly all the comedies have something of a tragic strain about them. Shakespeare was all of a piece . . . and the best commentary upon any one of his plays is furnished by all the others . . .

It would seem . . . that Shakespearian comedy differs, possibly fundamentally, from the comedy of most of the other comic dramatists in modern literature. In what does that difference consist? A cursory examination of the qualities which the comedies of these dramatists possess or display and those of Shakespeare do not, may help us to arrive at some useful preliminary conclusions . . .

Most modern comedy, from the 'comical satires' of Ben Jonson down to the plays of Ibsen and Bernard Shaw . . . has been critical in purpose. The means and the object of attack have differed. Jonson lashes typical crimes and follies of the period . . . Ibsen and Shaw expose, the one with mordant irony and the other with ridicule and brilliant wit, the conventions of a dying civilization and the hollow men of an outworn system of public life.

Shakespeare knows hardly anything of this . . . Closely connected with the lack of social criticism in Shakespearian comedy is the fact that he laughs, or gets his audience to laugh, quite as often *with* his characters as *at* them. High spirits is one of the predominant notes of his happy plays. His principal characters often find themselves in absurd situations, and sometimes do ridiculous things, but though we laugh, *they* usually laugh too; and their escapades are performed to the accompaniment of such a running commentary of witty dialogue that we are kept perpetually admiring as well as smiling at them . . . In modern or neo-classical comedy, on the other hand, we are usually invited to laugh at or even to scorn the chief characters. Indeed, such plays are frequently without a single character that evokes our admiration or our sympathy. Except in Shaw they tend to be grim; Shakespeare's tend to be gay.

It is true that two leading figures, Shylock and Malvolio, cannot be so described and that among minor characters Shakespeare often gives us butts to be laughed at. Yet even they are seldom lacking in some trait or some final speech which reveals them and excites our sympathy, while it is remarkable that if they are laughed at, they are laughed at by other characters in the play as well as by the audience. Laughter on the stage is, in fact, one of the marks of Shakespearian comedy.

The importance of the Clown in relation to all this is obvious. The Clown or Fool had a long stage-history behind him when Shakespeare took him over. But Shakespeare brought him to perfection, and after Shakespeare he disappears and is seen no more in the theatre, or in literature . . . The Fool is fundamental to Shakespearian comedy—not only because Costard, and Launce, and Lancelot Gobbo, and Bottom, and Touchstone, and Feste furnish the very salt of the plays in which they appear, but also because they symbolize and embody what is one of the outstanding features of Shakespearian comedy in general. They are at once butts and critics, as the 'allowed Fool' had always been at court and in castle throughout the Middle Ages . . . The Fool was an institution . . . which made a particular appeal to the mind of Shakespeare . . . and he clung to it even after he had passed from comedy to tragedy. The subtlest and tenderest of all fools is the Fool of *King Lear*, and the part he plays in the greatest of the world's tragedies will help us to understand his significance in the comedies.

In the Fool, I suspect, we come very close to Shakespeare's own standpoint as a comic dramatist. The idea that the deepest and greatest things in life may be hidden from the wise and prudent and be revealed to children and fools; that however much the stupid and the simple may be overwhelmed by confusion and ignominy in the court of the world's laughter, they are allowed the right of appeal to a higher court; and that what counts . . . is not rank or wealth or intellect, but humanity, native and unassuming; all this . . . forms the undertone, or one of the undertones, in Shakespeare's comedies. In other words, they appeal not to the intellect, but to what we call, for want of a better name, the heart . . .

From *Shakespeare's Happy Comedies*, Chapter I ('The Neglect of Shakespearian Comedy; His Comic Genius'), 1962.[5]

E. M. W. TILLYARD (1889–1962)

The question of the epic and how far Shakespeare took into account the contemporary ideas of the epic brings with it the general interpretation of the whole series of Shakespeare's Histories. At one time I followed a common opinion in looking on them less as self-sufficient dramas than as experiments in a solemn mode leading him to his true goal of tragedy. Men thought of Shakespeare caught up in his youth by the new and exciting self-realization of England, in a way deceived into thinking the political theme his true theme, lured on to picturing, as his climax, the perfect king, Henry V. Then, at the culminating moment he realizes that the man of action is not his real hero, that his imagined hero has let him down; and, schooled by this experience, he turns to the type of man who fundamentally attracts him, the man whose interests are private not public, whose sphere of thought is the universe and not the body politic. And, let down by his political hero, Shakespeare finds his true outlet in Brutus, Hamlet, and the other great tragic heroes.

I now think this scheme is wrong as a whole, though it contains elements of truth. First, Shakespeare turned the Chronicle Play into an independent and authentic type of drama, and no mere ancillary to the form of tragedy. He did this largely because he grasped the potentialities of the old Morality form, never allowing the personalities of his kings

[5] The writing of this book was originally contemplated in 1931.

to trespass on the fundamental Morality subject of Respublica. In the total sequence of his plays dealing with the subject matter of Hall he expressed successfully a universally held and still comprehensible scheme of history: a scheme fundamentally religious, by which events evolve under a law of justice and under the ruling of God's Providence, and of which Elizabeth's England was the acknowledged outcome. The scheme, which, in its general outline, consisted of the distortion of nature's course by a crime and its restoration through a long series of disasters and suffering and struggles, may indeed be like Shakespeare's scheme of tragedy; but it is genuinely political and has its own right of existence apart from tragedy. But in addition to this concatenated scheme, Shakespeare in *Richard II* and *1* and *2 Henry IV* gave us his version, which I have called epic, of what life was like in the Middle Ages as he conceived them and in his own day. The version was entirely successful and presents not even a parallel to the form of tragedy. It is one of Shakespeare's vast achievements and it stands unchallengeable: something entirely itself without a jot of suspicion that it ought to be, or ought to lead up to, something else; and achievement sufficient to put Shakespeare among the world's major poets. Nevertheless *Henry IV* led to *Henry V*, a play whose hero was no longer Respublica but Rex, and, once there was a change of hero, the form created by Shakespeare collapsed and the problem of tragedy thrust itself forward. Prince Hal had had nothing to do with tragedy and did not let his creator down; Henry V admitted the problems of tragedy and let his creator down very badly indeed. Thus it is that in a very minor and exceptional way, and at the very end of its exploitation, the History Play served as a transition to authentic tragedy. In *Macbeth* Shakespeare settled the adjustment of the political man of action to the other parts of the tragic world.

From *Shakespeare's History Plays*, 'Conclusions', 1946.

Examining the bare plots rather than the total impression of the last three plays, we find in each the same general scheme of prosperity, destruction, and re-creation. The main character is a King. At the beginning he is in prosperity. He then does an evil or misguided deed. Great suffering follows, but during this suffering or at its height the seeds of something new to issue from it are germinating, usually in secret. In the end this new element assimilates and transforms the old evil. The King overcomes his evil instincts, joins himself to the new order by an act of forgiveness or repentance; and the play issues into a fairer prosperity than had first existed.

The tragic events (for which Cymbeline's original error is ultimately responsible) are curiously apt to end in insignificance, while the new existence into which the tragic action issues is, as any recognizable and convincing way of life, a pallid and bloodless affair. By making an intellectual abstract of the plot we may convince ourselves that Cymbeline is regenerate at the end of the play; but from reading the play we can only say that he fails to stir our imagination and that his regeneration is a thing quite dead.

Perdita . . . is one of Shakespeare's richest characters; at once a symbol and a human being. She is the play's main symbol of the powers of creation. And rightly, because, as Leontes was the sole agent of destruction, so it is fitting . . . that the one of his kin whom he had thrown out as bastard should embody the contrary process. Not that Leontes, as a character, is the contrary to Perdita. *His* obsession is not a part of his character but an accretion. Her true contrary is Iago. It is curious that Iago should ever have been thought motiveless. The desire to destroy is a very simple derivative from the power-instinct, the instinct which in its evil form goes by the name of the first of the deadly sins, Pride. It was by that sin that the angels fell, and at the end of *Othello* Iago is explicitly equated with the Devil. Shakespeare embodied all his horror of this type of original sin in Iago. He was equally aware of original virtue, and he pictured it, in Perdita, blossoming spontaneously in the simplest of country settings. There is little direct reference to her instincts to create; but they are implied by her sympathy with nature's lavishness in producing flowers, followed by her own simple and unashamed confession of wholesome sensuality . . . The great significance of Perdita's lines lies partly in the verse, which (especially at the close) is leisurely, full, assured, matured, suggestive of fruition, and acutely contrasted to the tortured, arid, and barren ravings of Leontes, and which reinforces that kinship with nature and healthy sensuality mentioned above. But it lies also in the references to the classical Pantheon. The gods of Greece and Rome occur very frequently in the last plays of Shakespeare and are certainly more than mere embroidery. Apollo is the dominant god in *The Winter's Tale*, and his appearance in Perdita's speech is meant to quicken the reader to apprehend some unusual significance. He appears as the bridegroom, whom the pale primroses never know, but who visits the other flowers. Not to take the fertility symbolism as intended would be a perverse act of caution. Perdita should be associated with them, as symbol of the creative powers of nature, physical fertility, and of healing and re-creation of the mind. She is like Milton's youthful Ceres . . . or his Eve, mistress of the flowers of Paradise.

From *Shakespeare's Last Plays*, Chapter 2, 1938.

KENNETH MUIR (1907–)

Victorian critics tended to sentimentalize the comedies of Shakespeare's final period. They often assumed that the poet had emerged from the gloom of his tragic period to reach an 'ultimate mood of grave serenity', at peace with the world, and expressing his hopes for its future in the young lovers of the last plays. It was to counteract this sentimental attitude that Lytton Strachey wrote his notorious essay on 'Shakespeare's Final Period', in which he called attention to the many evil characters to be found in these plays, and argued that the poet at this time was bored with the theatre, bored with life, and bored with everything except his poetical dreams. Strachey's views were as absurd as the ones he sought to supersede, and critics of the past fifty years have sought to show that he was misguided. Some have shown that the existence of evil characters does not prove that Shakespeare was not concerned with reconciliation and forgiveness: it merely indicates that he was not escaping into a poetical utopia, where forgiveness and reconciliation would not be needed. Other critics have pointed to the theatrical mastery displayed in the plays—e.g., in the extraordinary last act of *Cymbeline*— which proves that he was still interested in the theatre. E. M. W. Tillyard argued that Shakespeare was seeking to complete the tragic cycle and to juxtapose 'planes of reality', so that, for example, he could in a single play make use of Holinshed's *Chronicles*, an Italian novel, a folk-tale, and the pastoral tradition. T. S. Eliot once suggested that Shakespeare had gone 'beyond the dramatic', that he was no longer interested in character for its own sake. Other critics have sought to explain the last plays by the changing fashions of the time and by the influence of Beaumont and Fletcher and Heywood.

It should be emphasized, on the one hand, that the first play of the series, *Pericles*, probably preceded the tragi-comedies of Beaumont and Fletcher, and that the romances have links with Shakespeare's earlier comedies; and, on the other hand, that he was trying to do something different from anything he had attempted before, devoting himself (in Keats's phrase) to 'other sensations'. Although the four romances resemble each other in several ways—they are all concerned, in one way or another, with reunion or reconciliation; they all impose a happy ending on a plot that could have ended in tragedy; three of them end with the reunion of parents, in two of them the reconciliation is cemented by the marriage of the children, and in three the sea plays a major role. Yet the plays also differ widely from each other: the hero of *Pericles* is unlucky; the hero of *The Tempest* is betrayed; the heroines of *The Winter's Tale* and *Cymbeline* are victims of jealousy; *The Tempest* obeys the unities of time and place, whereas *Pericles* and *The Winter's Tale* flagrantly disregard the unities to enable the daughters to grow to marriageable age; in two of the plays the hero repents and is forgiven by his wronged wife; and in *The Tempest* the wronged hero forgives his enemies.

In spite of the possibility of dividing the comedies into groups, therefore, it is more profitable to stress the differences between one comedy and another in the same group. Although all the comedies bear the mark of Shakespeare's hand, and although he repeated over and over again a number of favourite comic devices, each comedy was an attempt to do something different. Even the greatest is flawed, either by textual corruption or sheer carelessness, but each one is a unique experience.

The greatest change in critical opinion in the past sixty years related to the so-called 'problem' comedies. Most nineteenth-century critics—Pater being the outstanding exception—regarded them with embarrassment and distaste, assuming that Shakespeare was passing through a period of sex-nausea as the result of some unfortunate experience in his private life. But in the present century these plays have attracted more attention than any of the other comedies. This is partly because in their treatment of sex they are closer in spirit to modern literature than to nineteenth-century literature, and partly because their ambiguity makes them a more intersting topic for criticism than the earlier comedies, of which the meaning is not seriously in doubt.

The ending of *Measure for Measure*—the substitution of Mariana for Isabella in Angelo's bed, the Duke's pardon of Angelo, and Isabella's marriage—outraged Robert Bridges as it had Coleridge, because it ignored the claims of justice. It has been defended in the present century on two different levels: by W. W. Lawrence as a conventional conclusion which would be readily acceptable to the Jacobean audience, and by several later critics on theological grounds. G. Wilson Knight—in one of his earliest and best essays, published in 1930—stressed the scriptural affinities of the play; but he argued that Isabella, after failing to sacrifice her chastity to save her brother's life, was converted to a greater humanity by the example of Mariana. He was followed by J. Middleton Murry in his chapter on the play in *Shakespeare* (1936). These interpretations did not satisfy Una Ellis-Fermor, who regarded the play as cynical. R. W. Chambers . . . regarded the play as an essentially Christian treatment of forgiveness, and he defended Isabella's refusal to sacrifice her chastity—Shakespeare departed from all his sources in making her a novice—and her subsequent forgiveness of her enemy, Angelo. Muriel C. Bradbrook discussed Shakespeare's use of morality techniques; and Roy Battenhouse went even further in treating the play as an allegory, in which even the names of the characters are significant—Lucio, for example, being Lucifer. To Elizabeth M. Pope (*Shakespeare Survey 2*) Shakespeare was clarifying the ordinary Christian doctrine of the Renaissance and making a deliberate effort to harmonize the 'discrepancy between the conceptions of religious mercy and secular justice'. To J. C. Maxwell *Measure for Measure* is one of Shakespeare's most perfect works of art, and F. R. Leavis has also written on the greatness of the play.

On the other hand, several recent critics have reverted to the view that the play is in some sense a failure. T. M. Parrott speaks of the 'incongruity between the tragic theme, the tragi-comedy technique, and the realistic background'. E. C. Pettet speaks of a 'sour spirit of disillusionment and cynicism' in the play and a sense of strain in the artistry; E. M. W. Tillyard complains of 'an artistic breach of internal harmony' in the contrast between the two halves of the play; and Clifford Leech . . . is clearly uneasy at the attempts to make the play a theological allegory. This continuing debate at least exemplifies the complexity and vitality of the play, and the fascination it holds for recent critics. There is a greater measure of agreement on *All's Well that Ends Well*. The nineteenth-century view that Helena was contaminated by the sordid means she employed to obtain a prize of doubtful worth has given place to a realization that Shakespeare was dramatizing a tale of a heroine who fulfilled an apparently impossible task and that the Jacobean audience would cheerfully believe in Bertram's fifth-act repentance. To Bernard Shaw, Helena was a true Ibsenite character; to Wilson Knight she embodies qualities to be found in no other Shakespearian heroine; and to Muriel C. Bradbrook she exemplifies the theme that virtue is the true nobility.

From the *Introduction* to *Shakespeare: The Comedies*, Twentieth Century Views series, 1965 (sections V and IV).

Select Bibliography

WORKS:

PLAYS:

Scholarly editions of the individual plays are available in the *Arden* (Methuen) and *The New Shakespeare* (Cambridge University Press) editions. Many of the plays are also available in *A New Variorum Edition* (Dover Publications, New York).

POEMS:

The poems of Shakespeare are available in the *Arden* (Methuen) edition, edited by F. T. Prince.

BIOGRAPHY:

A Short Life of Shakespeare with the Sources abridged by Charles Williams from Sir Edmund Chambers' *William Shakespeare: A Study of Facts and Problems*, London: Oxford University Press, 1933.
A. L. Rowse, *William Shakespeare*, London: Macmillan, 1963.
Ivor Brown, *Shakespeare*, London: Collins, 1949. Also by Ivor Brown, *How Shakespeare Spent the Day*, London: Bodley Head, 1963.

CRITICISM:

Matthew Arnold, Preface to *Poems*, A New Edition, 1853.
A. C. Bradley, *Shakespearean Tragedy*, London: Macmillan, 1905.
— *Oxford Lectures on Poetry*, London: Macmillan, 1909.
E. K. Chambers, *William Shakespeare: A Study of Facts and Problems*, Vol. II, London: Oxford University Press, 1930. This contains the surviving criticism of Shakespeare, in prose and verse, by his contemporaries.
W. H. Clemen, *The Development of Shakespeare's Imagery*, London: Methuen, 1966.
S. T. Coleridge, *Coleridge on Shakespeare*, edited by Terence Hawkes, Harmondsworth: Penguin, 1969.
Edward Dowden, *Shakespeare: A Critical Study of his Mind and Art*, London: Routledge, 1875.
T. S. Eliot, *Selected Essays*, London: Faber, 1951.
Harley Granville-Barker, *Prefaces to Shakespeare*, 5 vols, London: Batsford, 1958–71.
William Hazlitt, *Characters of Shakespear's Plays*, London: Oxford University Press, 1817.
— *Lectures on English Poets*, London: Dent, 1818.
John Keats, *Letters*, edited by M. B. Forman, London, Oxford University Press, 1935.
G. Wilson Knight, *The Wheel of Fire*, London: Methuen, 1949.

— *The Imperial Theme*, London: Methuen, 1965.
— *The Shakespearian Tempest*, London: Methuen, 1953.
— *The Crown of Life*, London: Methuen, 1961.
— *The Mutual Flame*, London: Methuen, 1955.
L. C. Knights, *Explorations*, London: Chatto, 1946.
— *Some Shakesperaian Themes*, London: Chatto, 1959.
— *An Approach to Hamlet*, London: Chatto, 1960.
Charles Lamb, *Tales from the Tragedies of Shakespeare*, Bath: Brodie, 1927.
R. G. Moulton, *Shakespeare as a Dramatic Artist*, New York: Dover Publications, 1966.
Kenneth Muir, 'Introduction' in *Shakespeare: The Comedies*, Twentieth Century Views, Prentice-Hall, 1965.
Thomas De Quincey, 'On the Knocking at the Gate in *Macbeth*', 1823.
Walter Raleigh, *Shakespeare*, London: Macmillan, 1907.
George Saintsbury, 'Shakespeare: Life and Plays', *The Cambridge History of English Literature*, London; Cambridge University Press, 1910.
G. B. Shaw, *On Shakespeare*, edited by Edwin Wilson, Harmondsworth: Penguin, 1969.
D. Nichol Smith, *Eighteenth Century Essays on Shakespeare*, London: Oxford University Press, 1963. This contains most of the important Augustan criticism of Shakespeare, including Dr Johnson's 'Preface to Shakespeare' and Morgann's 'Essay on Falstaff'.
Caroline F. E. Spurgeon, *Shakespeare's Imagery and What It Tells Us*, London: Cambridge University Press, 1935.
E. E. Stoll, 'Art and Artifice in Shakespeare', *Hamlet: An Historical and Comparative Study*, New York: Gordian 1933.
E. M. W. Tillyard, *Shakespeare's Last Plays*, London: Chatto, 1938.
— *Shakespeare's History Plays*, London: Chatto, 1944.
— *Shakespeare's Problem Plays*, London: Chatto, 1950.
J. Dover Wilson, *The Essential Shakespeare*, London: Cambridge University Press, 1932.
— *What Happens in 'Hamlet'*, London: Cambridge University Press, 1951.
— *The Fortunes of Falstaff*, London: Cambridge University Press, 1943.
— *Shakespeare's Happy Comedies*, London: Faber, 1969.

ADDITIONAL RECOMMENDED READING:

Shakespeare Criticism, 1935–60, selected by Anne Ridler, London: Oxford University Press, 1970.
Shakespeare: The Tragedies, Patterns of Literary Criticism, edited by Clifford Leech, Chicago: University of Chicago Press, 1966.
Studies in Shakespeare, selected by Peter Alexander, London: Oxford University Press, 1964.